Ripley's Believe It or Not!®

Vice President, Licensing and Publishing Amanda Joiner

Editorial Manager Carrie Bolin
Editor Jordie R. Orlando
Text James Proud, Geoff Tibballs, Jordie R. Orlando
Proofreader Rachel Paul
Special thanks to Jessica Firpi and John Graziano

Designers Mary Eakin, Jordie R. Orlando
Reprographics Bob Prohaska
Cover Artwork Mary Eakin, Jordie R. Orlando

Library of Congress Control Number: 2018963946
ISBN 978-1-60991-219-2 (USA)
ISBN 978-1-84794-850-2 (UK)

First published in Great Britain in 2019 by
Random House Books

Random House Books
20 Vauxhall Bridge Road
London SW1V 2SA

www.penguin.co.uk

Random House Books is part of the Penguin Random
House group of companies whose addresses can be found
at global.penguinrandomhouse.com

A CIP catalogue record for this book is available from
the British Library.

For more information regarding permission, contact:
VP Intellectual Property
Ripley Entertainment Inc.
7576 Kingspointe Parkway, Suite 188
Orlando, Florida 32819
publishing@ripleys.com
www.ripleys.com/books

Manufactured in China in December 2018 by Leo Paper
First Printing

PUBLISHER'S NOTE
While every effort has been made to verify the accuracy
of the entries in this book, the Publisher cannot be held
responsible for any errors contained in the work. They
would be glad to receive any information from readers.

WARNING
Some of the stunts and activities are undertaken by experts
and should not be attempted by anyone without adequate
training and supervision.

Ripley's Believe It or Not!

100 Best Believe It or Not Stories

Ripley
PUBLISHING

a Jim Pattison Company

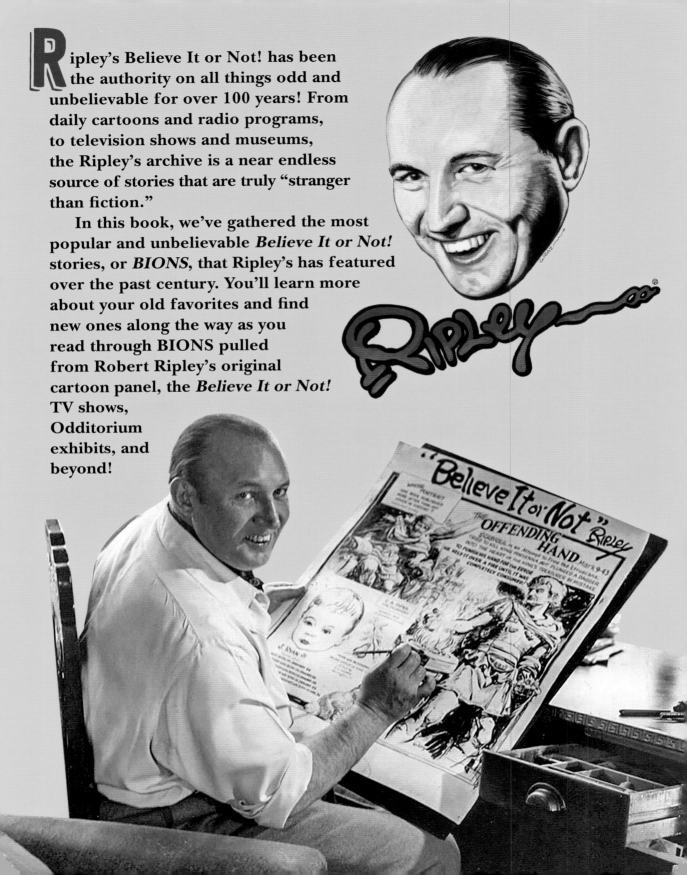

Ripley's Believe It or Not! has been the authority on all things odd and unbelievable for over 100 years! From daily cartoons and radio programs, to television shows and museums, the Ripley's archive is a near endless source of stories that are truly "stranger than fiction."

In this book, we've gathered the most popular and unbelievable *Believe It or Not!* stories, or *BIONS*, that Ripley's has featured over the past century. You'll learn more about your old favorites and find new ones along the way as you read through BIONS pulled from Robert Ripley's original cartoon panel, the *Believe It or Not!* TV shows, Odditorium exhibits, and beyond!

CHAPTER 1

Classics

Featured in:
- 1933 Chicago World's Fair Odditorium
- 1936 Great Lakes Exposition Odditorium
- June 7, 1937 cartoon
- Odditoriums as a wax figure

When asked if he wished he had legs, Johnny Eck reportedly quipped, "Why would I want those? Then I'd have pants to press."

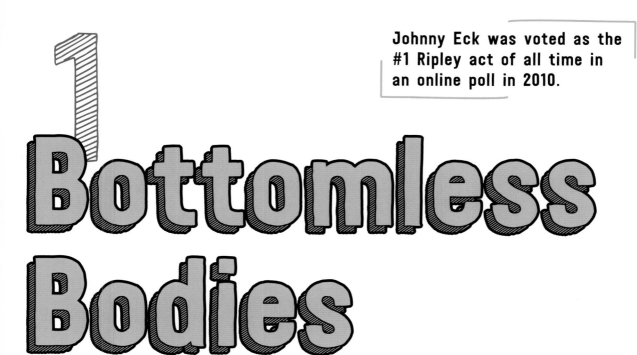

Bottomless Bodies

Johnny Eck was voted as the #1 Ripley act of all time in an online poll in 2010.

Billed as "The Most Remarkable Man Alive," John Eckhardt Jr., a.k.a. Johnny Eck, defied expectations his entire life. A twin, he was born 20 minutes after his brother Robert on August 27, 1911, in Baltimore, Maryland. While Robert was an average baby, Johnny was born with virtually nothing below his ribcage, resulting in him being less than 8 in (20 cm) long and weighing 2 lb (0.9 kg) at birth.

This hardly slowed him down. He began walking on his hands before his brother was even standing, and both boys showed an early aptitude for art. Johnny entered the sideshow world at age 12, Robert his constant companion. Their most legendary act consisted of Johnny chasing a pair of legs (actually a dwarf hidden in a special pair of pants) around the stage after being "sawed in half" by a magician. They would run backstage, where they would be replaced by Robert, who would appear in front of the audience, seemingly whole again, and loudly threaten to sue the illusionist.

Johnny famously appeared in Tod Browning's 1932 horror film, *Freaks*, as Half Boy. Soon afterward he could be seen at Ripley's Believe It or Not! Odditoriums at the 1933 Chicago World's Fair and the 1936 Great Lakes Exposition in Cleveland, Ohio, earning enough money to keep from losing his childhood home during the Great Depression.

Johnny and Robert would eventually retire and move back into that very same Baltimore house in which they were born. They were heavily involved in their community; the brothers built and operated a miniature train for the neighborhood

Johnny Eck continues to inspire to this day. Here is sideshow performer Short E. Dangerously recreating Eck's famous one-arm balance, plus his own bowling ball handstand stunt.

Featured in:
- **2017 book *Shatter Your Senses!***

children and Johnny returned to his love of art, becoming a window-screen painter. He passed away at the age of 79 on January 5, 1991, in the same house he was born.

There have been other "half-people" since Johnny Eck—notably Rose Siggins and Short E. Dangerously, both of whom have been featured in various Ripley's Believe It or Not! media. Rose appeared in the first episode of the 2000 revival of the *Ripley's Believe It or Not!* TV show, as well as in the 2007 book, *The Remarkable Revealed.* She was especially extraordinary due to the fact that she gave birth to two children with fully formed bodies. Sadly, she passed away in 2015 at the age of 43.

Short E. Dangerously (a.k.a. Aaron Wollin) was featured prominently in the 2017 book *Shatter Your Senses!* with an exclusive interview and photo shoot. Unlike Eck, one of his personal heroes, Short E. was born with legs, but they were amputated when he was two years old. Short E. travels extensively with a sideshow troupe, wowing audiences with acts similar to what Johnny did in the 1930s, but he's also got many of his own extreme stunts, like performing handstands on bowling balls and jumping from a chair onto a pile of flaming glass without being harmed.

Featured in:
- **Ripley's Believe It or Not! TV show in 2000**
- **2007 book *The Remarkable Revealed***

Rose Siggins at the premiere screening of the TV show *American Horror Story: Freak Show,* in which she played the character Legless Suzi.

2 Unofficial Anthem

Robert Ripley is remembered as a key figure in American popular culture for his outrageous claims and far-flung travels. Less well known is the cartoonist's role in helping "The Star Spangled Banner" become the official national anthem of the United States.

The words to the anthem were written by lawyer Francis Scott Key while detained on a British ship during the 1814 naval assault on Baltimore in the Anglo-American War of 1812–15. When the bombardment ended, Key was so moved by the sight of a giant stars and stripes flag still flying over Fort McHenry that he was inspired to compose a verse in tribute. Ironically, he decided that the words should be sung to the tune of "To Anacreon in Heaven," a popular British tune at the time. The English original was a bawdy drinking song from the 18th century that had gained popularity with American soldiers fighting in the Civil War. By the late 19th century, it had become the official anthem of the U.S. military—but not yet of the country itself.

Robert Ripley was always one to spot surprising contradictions and facts that, while technically correct, were hard to believe. In November 1929, he declared in his newspaper cartoon, "Believe It or Not! America has no national anthem." He was correct, of course, but the cartoon caused an uproar, and Ripley received so many angry letters from patriotic readers that he suggested they petition Congress instead. Five million Americans signed a petition to persuade Congress to declare the song the country's official song, and their voices were heard. In 1931 President Hoover signed legislation to adopt "The Star Spangled Banner" as the official anthem of the United States.

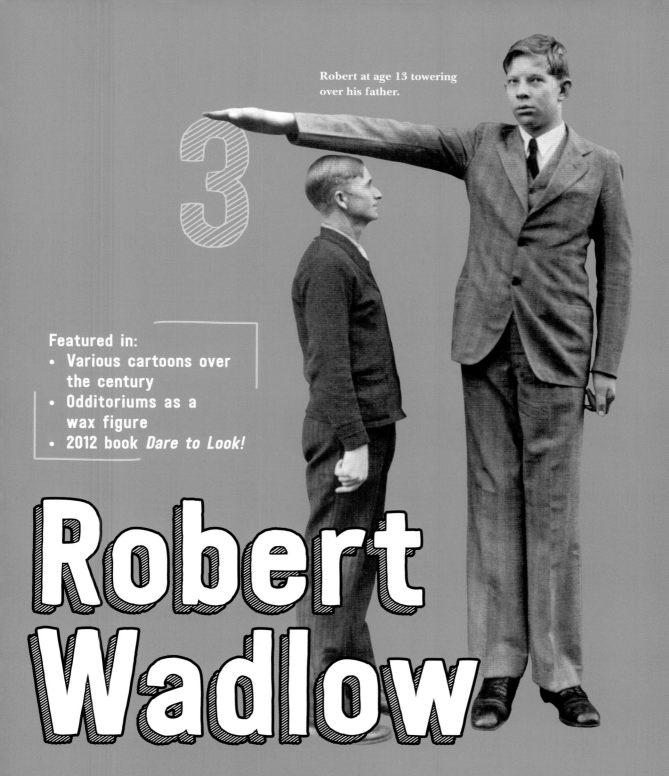

Robert at age 13 towering over his father.

3

Featured in:
- Various cartoons over the century
- Odditoriums as a wax figure
- 2012 book *Dare to Look!*

Robert Wadlow

Robert Wadlow, born February 22, 1918, in Alton, Illinois, was a normal-sized baby, weighing 8 lb 6 oz (3.8 kg) at birth, but by the time he was eight years old, he was taller than his father Harold, who stood 6 ft 2 in (1.88 m) tall.

He was so big that his school had to make a custom desk to fit his legs. At the age of 13, Wadlow became a 7 ft 4 in (2.2 m) Boy Scout, and his custom uniform required 14 yd (13 m) of material. At his tallest, the "Alton Giant" was 8 ft 11 in (2.72 m). The tallest man alive today, Sultan Kösen of Turkey, is a full 8 inches shorter.

In 1929, Robert Ripley drew Robert Wadlow for his Believe It or Not! cartoon with the caption, "the 11-year-old boy who wears a size 25 shoe." Word of the young "Illinois Giant" soon spread, and he embarked on a tour of America with his father, visiting 800 towns.

When the pair traveled by car, Wadlow would sit in the back with the front passenger seat removed to make room for his legs. His feet were so big—thought to be the largest ever—that he required shoes almost 20 in (50 cm) long, a U.S. size 37AA, costing as much as an average month's salary at the time.

As Wadlow became more famous, he appeared in adverts for a shoe company, who provided him with giant footwear as payment. When Robert Ripley opened his first permanent Odditorium in New York in 1939, a genuine pair of Wadlow's shoes was on display. The Alton Giant turned down various offers to appear in circus sideshows, which often featured much smaller "giants" of the time, but in 1937 he agreed to sign up with the famous Ringling Bros. Circus on the condition that he appear not in the sideshow but the main circus arena. He would make short, dignified cameo roles at famous venues such as Madison Square Garden, always wearing a smart suit tailored for his enormous frame.

Robert and Major Mite, a famous sideshow performer of the time, compare shoes sizes.

Wadlow's great height stemmed from an over-active pituitary gland that produced an abnormal amount of growth hormone. This meant that he never stopped growing, and at his heaviest he weighed almost 500 lb (227 kg). Wadlow's size and busy schedule took a toll on his health, and as a 21-year-old he already had braces on his legs and walked with the aid of a cane.

One year later, in 1940, he died from an infection caused by blisters from his leg braces. His family, fearful of grave robbers, requested that his coffin be lined with concrete. The resulting 10-ft (3-m) casket was so heavy, weighing half a ton, that 12 pallbearers were required to carry it at his funeral. Wadlow died one month after being measured at almost 9 ft (2.7 m) high, the tallest person to have ever lived.

Several of Robert Wadlow's shoes can be found in Ripley's Odditoriums around the world.

4
El Fusilado

Featured in:
- June 27, 1935 cartoon
- Radio show on July 16, 1937
- 1937 Cleveland Odditorium

On March 18, 1915, during the Mexican Revolution, a young fighter called Wenseslao Moguel was captured by enemy forces and sentenced to death by firing squad. At 5:00 p.m. that day, Moguel was lined up against a church wall in Halacho with several other captives and shot by nine executioners.

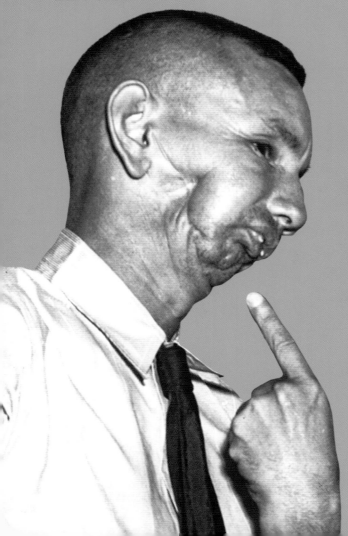

As the smoke cleared, an officer administered a bullet to each head with his pistol to make sure that none were left alive. As the bodies were cleared the next day, one of the prisoners was still breathing. Moguel had been shot nine times—including a coup de grâce to the face—but he was alive. He was pulled from the pile of corpses, given medical attention, and eventually freed. Perhaps his captors decided that he had suffered enough. Word spread of his unbelievable story, and he became known as "El Fusilado—The Executed One."

In June 1935, Robert Ripley featured El Fusilado in the Believe It or Not! cartoon, declaring "although horribly scarred, he is alive today and well in mind and body." In July 1937, Ripley flew Moguel 2,000 mi (3,200 km) from his home in Mexico to Radio City, New York, to be featured on his CBS show and appear at the Ripley's Odditorium in Cleveland. Wenseslao was pictured with Ripley to mark the occasion, and as Ripley had said, his contorted face bore terrible witness to the injuries that would have killed him on any other day.

5 Lighthouse Man

Using a 7-in (18-cm) lighted candle inserted in his head, the Lighthouse Man would act as a human lantern in the unlit alleys of Chunking, China, in the 1930s. He had cut a hole through the bone in his scalp so the candle could be held in place with sealing wax.

Featured in:
- Odditoriums as a wax figure
- 1931 book *The New Believe It or Not!*

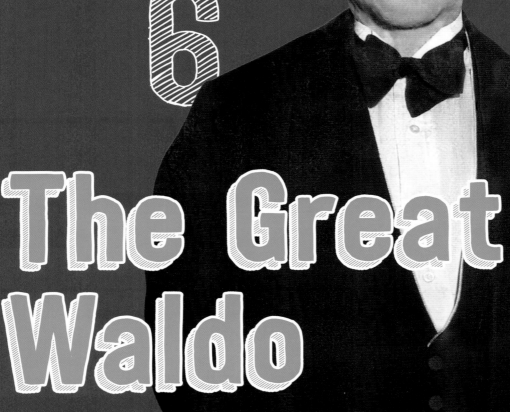

6

The Great Waldo

Dagmar Rothman, or The Great Waldo, specialized in bizarre acts of regurgitation. He could put a real live mouse in his mouth, swallow it, and open his mouth to show the audience that it really had been swallowed. Then he would somehow bring the creature up from his stomach in one piece, and let it crawl out of his mouth, totally unharmed.

While the mouse was swallowed, Rothman would proceed to light and smoke a cigarette, claiming that the smoke helped to pacify the rodent.

Rothman was also known as "The Regurgitating Geek." In sideshow lingo, a "geek" was someone who would swallow bizarre objects for entertainment. Rothman differentiated himself by bringing back up what he had already swallowed.

He would swallow and bring up various items belonging to audience members, including keys, coins, watches—inviting its owner to listen to the timepiece ticking in his stomach. He even swallowed fish, taking care to swallow plenty of water so that they didn't suffocate. He was so adept at controlling his throat and stomach muscles that he could swallow different colored balls, and regurgitate them in whichever order he liked. Perhaps The Great Waldo's most perplexing trick was to swallow a locked padlock, then a key, and regurgitate the padlock—unlocked.

Rothman performed around Germany and Austria in the 1930s, escaping to Switzerland when Hitler invaded Austria in 1938. An American talent agent saw his act one night and persuaded him to take his unique ability across the Atlantic. It was in the United States where Rothman found fame, performing at Ripley's Odditoriums and the Ringling Bros. Circus sideshows.

Other than "The Great Waldo," Rothman was also known as "The Regurgitating Geek" and "The Human Ostrich."

Rothman was always in formal wear, a stark contrast to his astonishing acts of regurgitation.

WORLD'S GREATEST FAKE

IN 1842, THE NEW YORK HERALD PRINTED A REPORT THAT DR. J. GRIFFIN OF THE "LONDON LYCEUM OF NATURAL HISTORY" HAD PASSED THROUGH MONTGOMERY, ALABAMA WITH "A MOST REMARKABLE CURIOSITY" A VERITABLE FIJI ISLAND MERMAID. THE ODDITY WAS PURCHASED IN CALCUTTA IN 1817 FOR $6,000° IT IS ACTUALLY A MONKEY'S HEAD AND CHEST, CLEVERLY SEWN TO A FISH'S BODY.

DR. GRIFFIN WAS A FAKE AND SO WAS THE MERMAID. THE WHOLE THING WAS ONE OF P.T. BARNUM'S GREAT HOAXS. WHEN THE FIJI MERMAID WAS FIRST DISPLAYED AT BARNUM'S AMERICA MUSEUM IN 1843.... HUNDREDS OF PEOPLE LINED UP TO SEE IT AT 25° A PEEP.

7
Fiji Mermaid

One of Robert Ripley's favorite exhibits, the Fiji "mermaid," is one of the most famous sideshow artifacts of all time. Its curious history dates back to the early 19th century, in the Dutch East Indies (modern-day Indonesia) where the mysterious beast was said to have been bought by a British sailor. The seller was the captain of a Dutch ship who claimed it was a genuine mermaid, obtained in China. The Englishman was so struck by the discovery that he paid an enormous sum of money to have it in his possession, reportedly selling his ship to meet the asking price. On his return to London in 1822, he put the creature on public display as "A Mermaid, the wonder of the world!"

There are several examples of Fiji mermaids in Odditoriums around the world.

In those days marine biology was somewhat limited, and many people believed it to be a genuine mummified mythical creature. Not everybody was convinced, however, and *The Times* of London called for the animal to be dissected, as long as it wouldn't be too badly damaged, so that its authenticity could be decided once and for all. The paper noted that the upper torso and head of the creature looked exactly like a baboon's, and the tail, the skin, and the fins resembled that of a regular salmon. They did add, however, that the figure was expertly constructed.

Sadly, the skeptics were correct—the mermaid was not a mythical creature but an ingenious hoax made from several apes (including possibly an orangutan and a baboon) and a fish, cleverly sewn together. Nevertheless, there was enough uncertainty about the real nature of the mermaid that it continued to attract visitors, and after being shown in London, it was taken on a tour of Britain.

After the captain's death, the mermaid was sold to another showman who brought it to the United States in 1842, where he persuaded the famous P. T. Barnum to put it on display at the American Museum in New York. Barnum charged 25 cents per viewing, and his advertising material claimed that the mermaid belonged to a respected British doctor who had discovered it in the Fiji islands in the South Pacific. The "doctor" gave serious scientific lectures in which he claimed the mermaid to be a missing link between humans and fish. In fact, the doctor was also a fake—he didn't exist; he was actually a character played by one of Barnum's assistants in order to make the mermaid seem more authentic. Any doubts raised over the mermaid's biology decades earlier in Britain had been forgotten, however, and the creature created a sensation. *The New York Sun* proclaimed, "We've seen it! What? Why that Mermaid!... the most odd of all oddities earth or sea has ever produced."

Barnum was still exhibiting the mermaid in the 1850s, but from that point on its history remains something of a mystery, and it was thought to have been lost in one of several fires that ravaged P. T. Barnum's collection. Many years later, Robert Ripley unearthed a similar mermaid in a shop in Macau, Asia, and exhibited it at his New York Odditorium in 1939, although he always maintained that it was a clever fake.

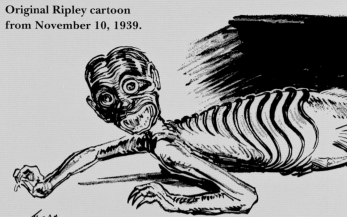

Original Ripley cartoon
from November 10, 1939.

The MERMAN of ADEN on the RED SEA
A FAKE THAT FOOLED EUROPEANS FOR CENTURIES!
SIR WALTER RALEIGH TOLD QUEEN ELIZABETH
OF HAVING SEEN ONE — AND THE CITY MUSEUM OF
MODENA, Italy, HAS A SPECIMEN THAT COST $25,000.00
IT IS NOTHING MORE THAN A CLEVER
COMBINATION OF A MONKEY AND A FISH

Ripley never portrayed
the Fiji mermaids in his
collection as real, saying
"I'm happy to say I've never
fooled my public. Not that
the public always thinks so."

Ripley and an usherette at the New York City
Odditorium pose with a Fiji mermaid in 1939.

8 Gurning Man

Featured in:
- September 8, 1933 cartoon
- 1933 Chicago World's Fair Odditorium
- Odditoriums as a wax figure

The Ripley's Odditorium at the 1933 Chicago World's Fair starred a man with the world's most remarkable face. J. T. Saylors was probably the finest ever exponent of "gurning," the art of facial contortion, a man whose flexible jaws enabled him to pull the funniest faces imaginable.

Saylors, of Villa Rica, Georgia, had previously received many offers of work from circuses and film producers, but his performance at the Odditorium was his first professional show. His appearance was publicized in the BION cartoon, where he was billed as a man who could "dislocate his jaws and swallow his nose." Gurning competitions are still taking place to this day, with the most famous being the World Gurning Championships held annually at Egremont, Cumbria, in England.

9

Featured in:
- The very first *Ripley's Believe It or Not!* book in 1929
- *Ripley's Believe It or Not!* TV show in 2002
- Odditoriums around the world

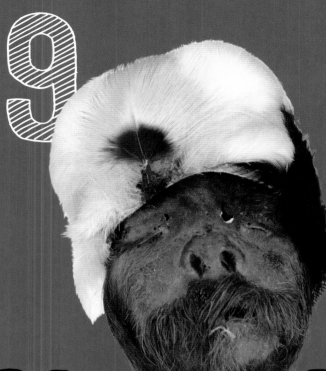

Shrunken Heads

Of all the artifacts associated with Robert Ripley and Believe It or Not!, the collection of genuine shrunken heads is probably the most famous. The discovery dates back to 1925, when Ripley made his first South American foray in a search for oddities to fill his cartoon and newspaper column. In Panama, he bought his very first shrunken head for $100, and unearthed the incredible story behind the remarkable creations that would become emblems of his Believe It or Not! empire.

The Jivaro tribes of Ecuador and Peru would take the head of a fallen enemy and subject it to a complicated process that eventually reduced it to the size of a fist. Tsantas, as the shrunken heads were known locally, were intended to protect the Jivaro from the vengeful souls of their victims. The lips and eyelids were sewn shut to prevent the spirits from escaping.

As Ripley recorded at the time of his visit, the practice seems to have continued well into the 20th century, fueled partly by tourists' desire for gruesome souvenirs. It's said that people were killed simply to keep up with demand. Ripley reported the story of a German scientist who went missing after venturing into the forest in an attempt to contact Jivaro headhunters. All that came out of the forest was a shrunken head with a red beard.

But it wasn't just heads that underwent mummified miniaturization, as one of

Part of the Ripley collection, this is one of six known female shrunken torsos to exist and was once owned by Ernest Hemingway.

Ripley's oddities proved; "Attaboy," as he called it, was a shriveled human body found by Ripley in Peru, only 6.5 in (16.5 cm) in height. Ripley also noted that the Museum of the American Indian in New York City had a South American shrunken figure in its collection, a man of regular height reduced to 31 in (79 cm). He was said to have been a Spanish officer who met a gruesome end while searching for gold in the Peruvian jungle.

For many years the exact process by which tsantas were produced was a mystery, but a 1960s era film shed some light on the subject. Made by a Polish film crew, it is remarkable on two accounts: Not only does it appear to suggest that the

Jivaro were still making shrunken heads at that time, it also provided never-before-seen footage of the head-shrinking process.

First, the Jivaro took a decapitated head and made an incision in the back of the scalp. Then they sliced the skin, flesh, and hair off the bone, ensuring that it remained intact. Next the scalp was boiled for several hours in a pot containing leaves high in tannins to clean it and start the shrinking process. Any remaining flesh was then scraped from the skin, and the head was dried with hot rocks and sand, shrinking it further. Then the skin was carefully pressed back into its original shape, the eyelids were sewn shut, and the mouth sealed with wooden pegs. Finally, the head was smoked over a fire for several days to complete the process of shrinking.

Modern laws against the transport of human remains eventually brought an end to the macabre practice of head shrinking, but Robert Ripley brought back several shrunken heads from his visits to South America, and in 1933 they were displayed at the first Odditorium at the Chicago World's Fair. When Ripley's first permanent museum opened in New York, a special cabinet was commissioned to house the collection. Today, these remarkable objects still hold a special place in several Ripley's museums.

There are more than 100 genuine shrunken heads in the Ripley collection.

Jivaro tribe members with a shrunken head, circa 1953.

THOMAS WEDDERS
A CIRCUS FREAK IN ENGLAND IN THE 1700s
HAD A NOSE 7½ INCHES LONG

10 Thomas Wedders

Thomas Wedders, who lived in Yorkshire, England, during the 18th century, had a nose that measured an incredible 7.5 in (19 cm) long. He was exhibited widely in an early form of traveling freak show.

11

Featured in:
- *Ripley's Believe It or Not!* books, cartoons, and events throughout the years

Sword Swallowers

It's thought that sword swallowing originated in India in 2,000 B.C., and sword swallowers have been a Ripley's Believe It or Not! favorite since Robert Ripley's very first Odditorium. The act of swallowing a sword remains one of the most challenging and gruesome circus acts, yet also one of the most fascinating.

In May 1933 at the Chicago World's Fair, Edna Price was one of the remarkable "human rarities and oddities" enlisted by Robert Ripley's talent spotters to appear at his show, where she would swallow 2-ft-long (0.6-m) neon tubes that glowed through her throat. Price had a sword-swallowing pedigree—her Aunt Maude had died after swallowing a sword for King George V of England in 1920.

Sword swallowing is as hard and dangerous as it looks, and it can take years to master the art. The first obstacle is the gag reflex, which is the body's way of saying that you shouldn't be sticking swords down your throat unless you really know what you're doing. Performers must have complete control of their body, keeping as still as possible, while also keeping the muscles of the throat totally relaxed as the sword passes through. Any tightening of the muscles involved could spell disaster.

Once the sword has eased its way down the esophagus, swallowers have to be careful not to let the blade damage the walls of the stomach—a potentially fatal injury. A popular complication is to swallow more than one sword, but this trick can spell even more danger due to the scissor-like slicing effect of multiple blades. Swords must also be kept in perfect condition, as any nicks on the blade could cause deadly bleeding.

At the 1934 return of Ripley's Odditorium to Chicago, Joseph Grendol swallowed seven blades at once. His wince-inducing signature trick was to swallow a 20-in (51 cm) bayonet attached to the butt of a rifle and then fire the gun. The danger of such a stunt was underlined by a more unfortunate performer two years later. Veteran sword swallower Bob Roberts would swallow the barrel of a 20-gauge shotgun and "fire" it by lighting gunpowder. The 61-year-old had performed the trick for 13 years until one night in 1936, when the explosion went terribly wrong at a carnival in Illinois. The recoil from the weapon ruptured a lung, causing fatal injuries.

Sword swallowing landmarks include Chayne "Space Cowboy" Hultgren's 28.5 in (72 cm) sword swallow. Chayne's stomach is unusually low in his body, enabling him to swallow

Joseph Grendol swallowing a bayonet attached to a rifle.

longer swords than any other performer. He has also swallowed an incredible 24 swords simultaneously. Other modern sword swallowers include Chris Steele of the vaudeville couple Captain and Maybelle, who can swallow a blade weighed down with cinderblocks, and Dan Meyer, who has performed at many Ripley events, including swallowing swords underwater at a Ripley's Aquarium!

Events celebrating World Sword Swallowers day have regularly been held at Ripley's Odditoriums around the world.

Captain swallowing a blade weighed down with cinder blocks on each side.

Stills from archival footage of Edna Price, "Queen of Sword Swallowers," swallowing a glowing neon tube.

Featured in:
- The first *Ripley's Believe It or Not!* book in 1929
- August 23, 1929 cartoon
- *Ripley's Believe It or Not!* TV show in 2002
- 2004 *Ripley's Believe It or Not!* book
- Odditoriums as a wax figure

12

Stretched Necks

Robert Ripley first encountered "long-necked" women on his travels in Southeast Asia in the 1920s. Today the women can still be found, but the practice is not quite what it seemed to early explorers like Ripley.

The Kayan woman of Myanmar have brass rings added to their necks from the age of five or six, forcing the head further from the body. The heavy adornments are actually long, straight coils wound round the neck in a painstaking process that can take hours. As the girl grows, more coils might be added, until she could be wearing 20 lb (9 kg) of metal around her throat, giving the impression of an elongated neck that stretches as much as 15 in (38 cm) from the body.

The original reasons behind the unusual tradition have long been forgotten, but theories range from the simple (an ideal of beauty that prizes a long neck), to the mystical (the idea that the long necks resemble that of a dragon's), to the practical (to give young girls added protection from tiger attacks). The practice continues to this day, although as secretive Myanmar modernizes, it is gradually dying out. Neck

Despite appearances, their necks are not actually stretched. Rather, their shoulders have been pushed down at an extreme angle.

rings are not compulsory, and many Kayan girls now choose not to be fitted.

Although it appears as though the necks of Kayan women have been literally stretched, the vertebrae are still intact. X-rays of Kayan women who have worn coils for years show that it is instead the collarbones and ribs that deform, being bent gradually downward until the shoulders slope at an extreme angle, giving the illusion of an incredibly long neck. This is why the notion that a Kayan woman would die of a broken neck if all her coils were removed is a commonly repeated myth. Kayan women do wear their rings at all times, even when asleep, but they are occasionally removed for cleaning with few ill effects.

13

Heavy Lifters

Bill Steed ran one of the world's most unusual schools, Croaker College, founded in 1972 in Sacramento, where for many years he taught frogs to jump further using his "learn-while-you-sleep" hypnosis technique.

The "Professor," as he was known, initially only trained humans with his sleep training, but after attending the annual frog jumping contest in Calaveras County, California, he had a thought: "I could motivate people. Why not motivate frogs, too?" Soon Steed had awarded himself a D.F.P. (Doctorate in Frog Psychology) and was running "the only institution of higher learning for frogs."

The six-week course cost $50 per frog, which included a rigorous exercise regime, massage, saunas, swimming (naturally), and hundreds of hours of psychological training under hypnosis. The amphibian workouts included a high-dive from a 30-in (76-cm) board into a paddling pool, chin-ups to develop the front legs, and bench-pressing with tiny balsa wood barbells. While the frogs slept, Steed played recordings of positive affirmations that he also used on his human clients. The idea was that the frogs (and the humans) would absorb this information more effectively while in the dream state. Steed was once asked by a visiting journalist from *Sports Illustrated* whether his frogs could understand the recordings. "Dogs understand English, why not frogs?" he replied.

Croaker College could claim to have some famous alumni, including frogs belonging to Dolly Parton, Johnny Carson (Steed and his frogs once performed on *The Tonight Show*), Johnny Cash, and even President Reagan. The professor boasted that six of his stable had gone on to take first place in the prestigious Calaveras contest, an event that marked Mark Twain's 1865 short-story *The Celebrated Jumping Frog of Calaveras County*.

Mule-Faced Woman

Grace McDaniels was born in 1888 in Iowa, with the birthmark that would define her career. As an adult, her face was swollen with protuberances and extremely large lips, creating a striking countenance that earned her an unfortunate moniker: "the ugliest woman in the world."

Featured in:
- 1933 Chicago World's Fair Odditorium
- 2011 book *Strikingly True*
- Odditoriums as a wax figure

After winning an "ugliest woman" competition in the 1920s, McDaniels joined a traveling sideshow and began a successful entertainment career. She would climb the sideshow platform wearing a heavy veil and only show her face after a build-up from the master of ceremonies, who told the waiting audience, "You will see the mule-faced woman, Grace McDaniels, the only living lady in all the world who was born with the face of a mule." When Grace finally removed the veil—which she didn't wear offstage—it's said that men and women would faint at the sight of her deformity. Nevertheless, she preferred to be called the "mule-faced woman," rather than the "ugliest woman in the world," and that's how she became known.

McDaniel's unusual appearance is thought to have been caused by the rare congenital disorder Sturge-Weber syndrome, which causes deforming birthmarks. She would tour for decades as the Mule-Faced Woman, but perhaps her biggest gig was performing at the first Ripley's Believe It or Not! Odditorium, at the 1933 Chicago World's Fair.

Despite her unusual appearance, Grace did not lack for romantic attention, and had a son called Elmer, who later became her manager. She would spend winters in Gibsonton, Florida, renowned as a town where traveling sideshow and circus performers spent the off-season. Grace shared the town with many well-known performers, including Grady "Lobster Boy" Stiles, Al "The Giant" Tomaini, and Percilla the Monkey Girl. Today you can see Grace in Ripley's Odditoriums around the world, as she is one of several famous performers immortalized in a waxwork figure.

One of the many wax figures of Grace McDaniels featured in Ripley's Odditoriums.

The Mighty Atom could bend steel bars with apparent ease, shocking those who would judge him by his size.

Featured in:
• July 1, 1931 cartoon
• 2014 book
  Reality Shock

Pound for pound, the Mighty Atom may have been the strongest man in the world.

15 The Mighty Atom

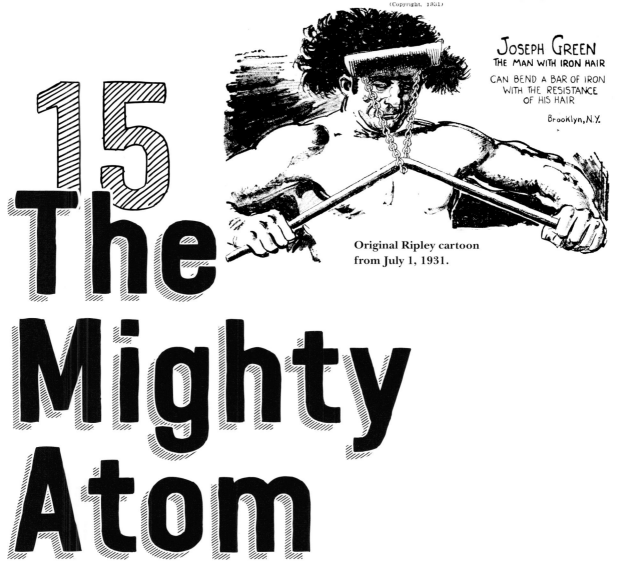

JOSEPH GREEN
THE MAN WITH IRON HAIR

CAN BEND A BAR OF IRON
WITH THE RESISTANCE
OF HIS HAIR

Brooklyn, N.Y.

Original Ripley cartoon
from July 1, 1931.

Ripley's Believe It or Not! has featured some remarkable feats of strength over the years, but no strongman had as much of an impact as Joseph "The Mighty Atom" Greenstein. Standing only 5 ft 4 in (1.6 m) and weighing around 150 lb (68 kg), Joseph Greenstein might not have stood out in a crowd, but his feats of strength distinguished him from even the heaviest strongmen to have been featured by Ripley's. Pound for pound, The Mighty Atom may have been the strongest man in the world.

Joseph Greenstein was born in Poland in 1893, and was reportedly a sickly child. One day he visited a touring circus, where a Russian wrestler and circus strongman noticed something in the young boy, and helped transform him from small and weak into a pocket-powerhouse wrestler.

The young Greenstein even accompanied the Russian on tour to learn the art of the strongman. He visited Asia and studied martial arts, becoming interested in developing the mind as well as the body. He would credit the mental powers that he learned in the Far East as being the true source of his great strength. Greenstein later arrived in the United States, finding work in the Texas oilfields.

While living in Houston, his remarkable physical capabilities made the news after a bizarre accident in which he was shot in the head by a friend's pistol. Luckily, his skull was so strong that the bullet was flattened and did not penetrate the bone.

Later Greenstein bought a gas station, where he got his big break. It's said that Houdini pulled up with a flat tire one day, and after Greenstein changed it for a new one with his bare hands, the legendary magician suggested that he might have a future in show business.

Joseph Greenstein became The Mighty Atom, and he moved to the Bronx in New York City, where he mastered creative feats of strength that belied his diminutive stature. He could lift 500 lb (227 kg) weights with his teeth, bend iron bars using his hair, bite nails and steel chains in half, and tie horseshoes in knots. Greenstein also became something of a local hero after single-handedly fighting off a gang of Nazis who were terrorizing his neighborhood.

The Atom wowed audiences at Atlantic City and Coney Island, and regularly appeared in Ripley's Believe It or Not! During each performance he would send one of his children into the audience to sell a special tonic that he claimed was the secret to his strength.

Greenstein preparing to break a metal chain across his chest.

The Mighty Atom Jr. pulling a car with his teeth at 92 years old.

In 1934 he had a rare accident, breaking a rib during a performance in New York City. He had bitten a nail in two and bent an iron bar with his hair, and then while attempting to lift a 100 lb (45 kg) dumbbell over his head, the strain proved too much and he broke a rib. When the ambulance arrived he declined a ride, declaring instead that would pull the vehicle to the hospital with his hair.

But perhaps the most remarkable aspect of Greenstein's story is not the feats of strength themselves, but how long he was able to perform them. At an age when other strongmen would have long since retired from the iron game, The Mighty Atom was still bending iron bars and breaking chains with his chest.

In 1974, he performed at a martial arts exhibition at Madison Square Garden at the age of 92. He died three years later, demonstrating his powers to the end.

Other Mighty Atom feats included lying on a bed of nails with the added weight of 17 band members and their instruments on top of him, pulling a 32-ton truck, and inviting people to try and bend iron bars over his nose. In 1928 he prevented a plane that was tied to his hair from taking off at Buffalo Airport, New York. Greenstein is thought to have been the inspiration for the DC Comics character Atom, who first appeared in 1940.

He had 10 children, and his son Mike also became a strongman: The Mighty Atom Jr., specializing in feats of strength using his teeth. The Mighty Atom Jr. certainly inherited his father's longevity—in 2014 he appeared on TV pulling a car with his teeth in his early 90s.

Featured in:
- December 8, 1929 cartoon
- 1934 Chicago World's Fair Odditorium
- 2004 *Ripley's Believe It or Not!* book
- Odditoriums around the world

16
Art Imitates Life

One of Robert Ripley's most treasured possessions was a wooden statue carved by the Japanese artist Hananuma Masakichi, completed in the 1880s. The artwork was a life-sized self-portrait, said to have been started by Masakichi after he was diagnosed with tuberculosis. It was for his wife, so that she had something to remember him by when he succumbed to the illness.

ut this was no ordinary self-portrait. What attracted Ripley was the obsessive precision and dedication of the artist in replicating himself down to the finest detail. In creating the sculpture, Masakichi glued together thousands of wooden strips, then stood in front of a mirror and carved every single detail of his naked body into the wood, from the ripples of his muscles to his veins, and even his body hair, which was plucked from his own head and placed in thousands of tiny holes in the wood, like real hair follicles. It is said that Masakichi even used his fingernails and teeth to complete the eerie replication. Incredibly lifelike, it was hard to distinguish the artwork from the model. When the sculpture was exhibited, the artist would stand next to it in a matching pose, challenging the

Ripley enjoyed pranking visitors to his house by hiding the statue and waiting for them to find it.

audience to work out which Masakichi was the real one.

In 1934, Robert Ripley bought the sculpture from an antiques shop in San Francisco, declaring it "the greatest piece of art in the world." He put it on display in the 1934 Odditorium at the Chicago World's Fair, and it traveled with the Odditoriums around the United States as the jewel in the Ripley collection, before residing at Ripley's first permanent museum in New York in 1940. The original statue was damaged in the 1989 San Francisco earthquake, but after careful restoration, Masakichi was eventually back on display, and perfect copies can be seen at other Ripley museums around the world. Even the copies are so lifelike that they could be mistaken for Masakichi himself!

Man or statue? The Masakichi statue is currently on display in the Amsterdam Odditorium.

Featured in:
- Various cartoons throughout the century
- *Ripley's Believe It or Not!* TV show in 1984 and 2002
- 2011 book *Strikingly True*

17 Sadhus

In 1923, Robert Ripley traveled to India, where in the cities of Calcutta and Benares, he recorded seeing Hindu holy men sitting in "twisted postures of mystic contemplation." The men Ripley encountered were religious ascetics known as Sadhus who had removed themselves from normal life and survived on handouts.

There are still many sadhus in India today, and they gather at Hindu festivals such as the Kumbh Mela, held on the banks of the Ganges every four years. In devoting themselves to extreme feats of endurance and mental strength, sometimes for their entire lives, sadhus have mastered the practice of mind over matter in order to reach spiritual fulfilment. As Ripley noted, sadhus often demonstrate a complete indifference to pain; some may stick pins through their tongue, and one man claimed to have spent 12 years lying on a bed of nails.

A devoted sadhu might raise his arm aloft for years, until the limb withers and becomes frozen in that position. Some sadhus would refuse to sit or lie down for years at a time, even when asleep. Such physical hardships would provide

A sadhu who vowed never to lie down.

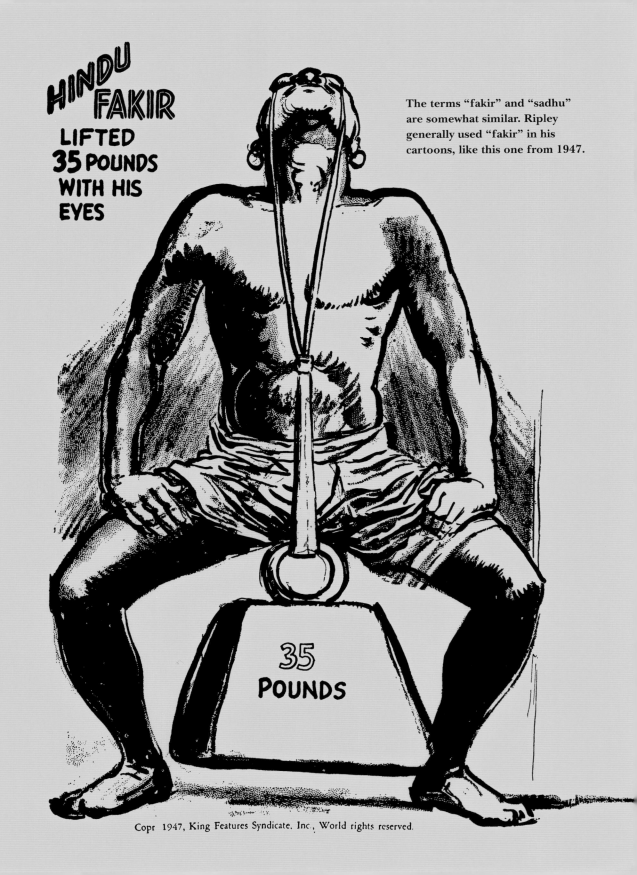

HINDU FAKIR
LIFTED 35 POUNDS WITH HIS EYES

The terms "fakir" and "sadhu" are somewhat similar. Ripley generally used "fakir" in his cartoons, like this one from 1947.

35 POUNDS

an opportunity for the sadhus to elevate their minds above worldly pain. Ripley photographed a sadhu in Calcutta who had his leg bent behind his head in a painful-looking yoga position. He had kept it there for so long that it became stuck, leaving his right foot forever resting on his left shoulder.

One of Ripley's cartoons from the time features a sadhu from Benares who held his hand in a fist for 12 years, until his fingernails grew through his palm. For Ripley's 1934 Odditorium, he brought Swami See Ram Lai over from India. The sadhu would stick pins through his tongue to help keep a vow of silence, and to show how he could handle the pain. On a later trip to the holy site of Bodh Gaya in 1936, Ripley encountered a man who had walked on all fours in tribute to the monkey god Hanuman for so long that he was unable to walk upright.

It's recorded that sadhus have buried their own heads in the ground for days at a time, breathing only through a tube. In 1837, the *Daily Telegraph* in London claimed that an Indian sadhu named Haridas had survived being buried alive for 40 days without food or water.

Unsurprisingly, such feats did not always end well. In 1925 *The Times* of London reported the case of Baba Dwarkapuri, a Hindu ascetic who allowed himself to be buried alive in a state of "suspended animation." By the time he was retrieved from the ground, he was dead. His disciples, who had dug the hole and filled it in, were charged with aiding and abetting suicide but later discharged.

Ripley once reported the story of a sadhu who rolled sideways from Lhassa, Tibet, to Benares, India, across the Himalayan Mountains. It sounds unbelievable, but modern-day sadhus are

Ripley with a "monkey man" sadhu at Bodh Gaya in 1936.

known to roll through towns to demonstrate their holiness. In 2004 a sadhu known as Lotan Baba, or "Rolling Baba," rolled for 2,485 mi (4,000 km) to the top of a mountain in Jammu, Northern India. He had rolled on his side for eight months, covering up to 10 mi (16 km) a day. Newspaper reports state that after becoming a mystic, Rolling Baba stood in one place for seven years, and he is now thought to have covered almost 20,000 mi (32,000 km) rolling on his side. In 2005, he tried to roll 1,500 mi (2,400 km) from India to Pakistan to promote peace between the two countries, but was stopped at the border because he didn't have a passport.

18

Double Vision

Believe it or not, Liu Ch'ung was born with double pupils in each eye!
Despite his abnormality, he became Governor of Shansi, China, and
Minister of State in 995 A.D. Later, through an affair with the Dowager
Empress, he had his son proclaimed heir apparent of all China!

HENRY HAWN
– of Mills, Ky.
HAS **2** PUPILS IN EACH EYE!

Although Liu Ch'ung's condition is extremely rare, other four-eyed men have been recorded by medical science. In 1931, Robert Ripley personally met a double-eyed man named Henry Hawn living in Mills, Kentucky!

Liu Ch'ung's distinctive appearance may have been the result of either pupula duplex (Latin for "double pupil") or polycoria. Pupula duplex is not yet a recognized medical condition and is so rare that some people doubt whether it actually exists. It is thought to occur when a genetic mutation causes someone to develop two irises, corneas, and retinas on the same eyeball.

Another Chinese ruler, Xiang Yu, a mighty warlord from the second century BC, was also said to have had the condition. It is no coincidence that two of the few people with pupula duplex became rulers, because in Chinese tradition it was seen as the mark of a king or a wise person.

The other plausible explanation was that Liu Ch'ung had polycoria, a very rare eye disorder where the iris has more than one pupillary opening. This can create the impression of two pupils.

Featured in:
- **The first *Ripley's Believe It or Not!* book in 1929**
- **Odditoriums as a wax figure**

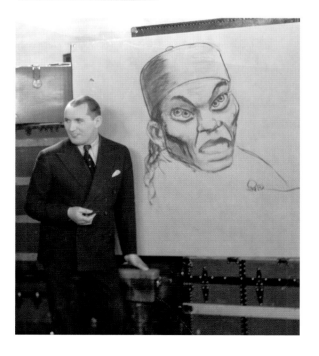

19
Jeremy Bentham

The British philosopher Jeremy Bentham (1748–1832) is best known for his pioneering work on the concept of utilitarianism. He lives on in a different way, however, at University College London. Bentham left orders that when he died his body should be dissected for the purposes of science, and his remains displayed for educational purposes: what he called his "Auto-Icon."

Featured in:
- 1927 cartoon
- The very first *Ripley's Believe It or Not!* book in 1929
- *Ripley's Believe It or Not!* TV show in 1981

Bentham desired that "the skeleton will cause to be put together in such a manner as that the whole figure may be seated in a chair usually occupied by me when living, in the attitude in which I am sitting when engaged in thought…" He also suggested that if his surviving friends should ever meet up to discuss the philosopher after his death, his Auto-Icon should be "conveyed to the room in which they meet."

Bentham had some unconventional ideas while he was alive, and this request was no different. It has been described as the first-ever instance of an individual donating their body to science. He quite reasonably thought his body would be more useful to the world above the ground than below it.

The philosopher was so involved in preparations for his own preservation that he selected the glass eyes to be used in his mummified skull and liked to carry them around in his pocket.

After Bentham's death at the age of 84, his body was dissected by a friend, Dr. Southwood Smith, in front of a group of the philosopher's associates. The event was recorded in *The Times* newspaper.

Bentham's head was then removed and subjected to a preservation process similar to that traditionally used by the Māori people, using smoke and sulphuric acid to dry the skull while preserving its features. His skeleton was dried, padded out with hay to resemble his body shape, and then dressed in one of his black suits, as he requested in his will, complete with a hat.

Bentham was finally laid to rest in a sitting position in a mahogany and glass display case, able to peer out at the observer. His body was originally entrusted to the care of Dr. Smith, but in 1850 it was received by University College London, and he is still there to this day on public display.

Bentham has been present at several official meetings of the College Council, where it's said that if the vote is tied, Bentham votes in favor.

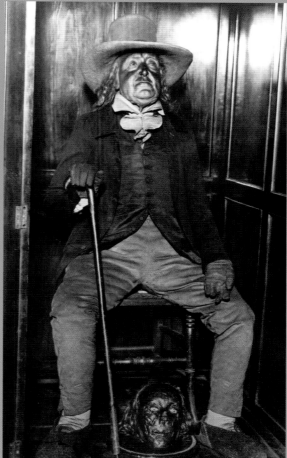

Before being locked away for safekeeping, Bentham's head sat at his feet.

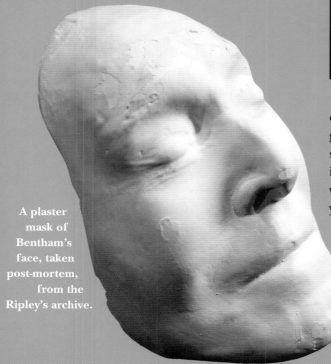

A plaster mask of Bentham's face, taken post-mortem, from the Ripley's archive.

Unfortunately, Bentham's head did not emerge from the preservation process in good enough condition for his "Auto-Icon," so a wax copy sits on his mummified shoulders instead. Bentham's real mummified head was displayed alongside his body for many years, but it attracted unwanted attention from student pranksters, and it has been stolen on a number of occasions.

In the 1970s, students from rival London school Kings College broke into the building where Bentham is kept, stole his head, and demanded a ransom be paid to charity. The relic is now kept locked away from mischievous undergraduates.

Acquitted by Sea

20

On the original *Ripley's Believe It or Not!* TV program in September 1940, Robert Ripley shared a story titled "Acquitted by Sea," in which he introduced a dramatized tale of remarkable coincidence that weaved personal misfortune into one of the 20th century's most famous tragedies.

Featured in:
- The original *Ripley's Believe It or Not!* show

In 1904 William Westover was working as a teller at a bank in New York City. One day he left his cage unattended to take a phone call from his girlfriend. When he returned to his station, thousands of dollars had been stolen. Although he had not taken the money, he was blamed by his manager and reported to the police. He was deemed legally responsible for the loss and sentenced to 10 years in jail.

Westover was released in 1910 on good behavior. After failing to find work, he reluctantly went back to the manager who had fired him. Although he wouldn't give Westover his old job back, he did give him a loan to help him travel to the United Kingdom for a fresh start.

Westover had no more luck in London; soon his loan money ran out and eventually he was reduced to living on the streets. He was arrested by the police as a vagrant and found himself back in court once again. He was declared an undesirable alien and sent back to America on the first ship to leave Southampton—the RMS *Titanic*.

Westover was locked in a prison cabin five decks down on the giant ship's maiden voyage across the Atlantic. On the fifth night, *Titanic* hit the infamous iceberg. As the ship took on water and started to sink, Westover wriggled his way through a porthole and leaped into the last lifeboat. As the survivors rowed away from the stricken vessel, they noticed a man fall from the top deck.

Westover pulled him from the water, and saw that it was his old boss. He was dying, but before he passed away, the bank manager admitted that it was he who had stolen the money from Westover's cage all those years ago. With the confession witnessed by his fellow survivors, Westover's name was cleared, and he was awarded $43,000 in compensation for the miscarriage of justice.

21 The Human Owl

Martin Laurello, born Martin Emmerling in Germany in the 1880s, had many names; he was also known as the Human Owl, or Bobby the Boy with the Revolving Head.

As a young man, he discovered an unnatural ability to rotate his head, and spent three years perfecting the trick. As the Human Owl, a regular feature on the European sideshow circuit, Laurello's head would swivel a full 180 degrees, so that he could look directly over his own back while walking forward. In his plain white shirt and slacks, The Human Owl probably failed to stand out among his more outlandish colleagues, but once his head started to turn, and keep turning, his remarkable abilities made audiences gasp. The sideshow barker would loudly proclaim that he was only able to swivel his head so far by dislocating several bones in

his neck! It's more likely that he was just extremely flexible.

Laurello later took his act across the Atlantic in 1921, where he performed for the famous Ringling Bros. traveling circus, Hubert's Museum in New York City, and at the famous Coney Island Dreamland fairground. In 1933, he was one of the stars to appear at the first-ever Ripley's Odditorium as part of the Chicago World's Fair. Ripley's performers proved to be great crowd-pullers, attracting over two million visitors. The Human Owl continued to be one of the biggest draws at Ripley's Odditoriums throughout the 1930s, and in 1940 he was one of the special guests pictured at a *LIFE* magazine party thrown by Robert Ripley at his island mansion in New York state.

22 Eye Poppers

Featured in:
- August 3, 1929 cartoon
- 2015 book *Eye-Popping Oddities*
- Odditoriums as a wax figure

Avelino Perez Matos was one of the earliest "eye poppers" featured in Ripley's Believe It or Not! He could bulge his eyes more than a centimeter out of their sockets at will, to the extent that it looked like his eyeballs would pop out at any moment.

In 1928, Robert Ripley learned about the man from Baracoa, Cuba, with an astonishing ocular talent, and he featured Matos in the Believe It or Not! cartoon a year later. When selecting remarkable individuals for the first Odditorium in 1933, Ripley brought Matos from Cuba to perform as the "The Human Eye Popper," and his photographs—and a lifelike waxwork figure—have adorned Ripley's museums ever since.

The ability to roll back the eyelids in such a manner is known in medical circles as *exophthalmos*, and can be a symptom of various diseases. Avelino, however, was perfectly healthy, and didn't even need glasses!

Some modern-day eye poppers were featured in the aptly-named book *Eye-Popping Oddities* and include Jalisa Thompson, who worked at the Atlantic City Odditorium, and brothers Hugh and Antonio Francis of Essex, England.

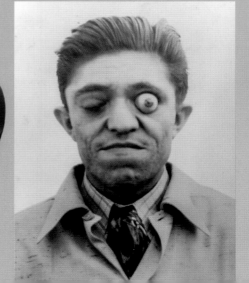

Featured in:
- 2006 book *Expect the Unexpected*
- September 5, 2009 cartoon
- 2018 episode of YouTube show *Cool Stuff Strange Things*

23 Headless Chicken

We've all heard the phrase, "running around like a chicken with its head cut off," but did you know that the bizarre image actually has some basis in reality?

On September 10, 1945, farmer Lloyd Olsen was slaughtering chickens on his farm in Fruita, Colorado. He selected a five-month-old Wyandotte rooster named Mike, and removed the chicken's head with a single axe blow. Unfortunately, or perhaps fortunately, Olsen's aim was awry, and although Mike's head had been removed, the rooster survived the blow. But not only was Mike not dead; he could still balance on a perch, walk around, and peck for food with a non-existent beak. He even made attempts at crowing. The rooster was so energetic despite his injury that the farmer couldn't bring himself to finish the job, instead putting him in a box to see what would happen.

The next morning Olsen was astounded to discover that Mike was still alive. He was so impressed with the rooster's resilience that he began caring for the disabled bird. He would feed Mike by squeezing liquidized food into the exposed neck using an eyedropper. A week later, Mike was still going strong. Olsen took the bird to market with him to impress his customers, and the story got around.

An entertainment agent persuaded Olsen to take Mike on the road as a sideshow attraction, and he was soon making money from members of the public who paid to see the amazing headless chicken. Olsen took Mike to the University of Utah to figure out what was keeping the rooster alive. It transpired that while the axe blade had severed the front of the head and the beak, it had missed the jugular vein and most of the brain. A blood clot

Sculpture of Mike the headless chicken in Fruita, Colorado.

prevented Mike from bleeding to death, and the remaining brain material was enough to support movement and vital mechanisms such as breathing. Mike's story soon spread nationwide, and photos of the bird standing next to his decapitated head were published in *LIFE* magazine. Sadly Mike's life on tour was not to last: he choked to death in an Arizona hotel room in 1947.

Nevertheless, Mike made such an impression in his short life that he was immortalized in a metal sculpture that still stands today in the center of Fruita, and the town's present-day residents remember him annually at the Mike the Headless Chicken festival. Attractions include a selection of chicken delicacies, a dance-like-a-chicken contest, "Pin the head on the chicken," and a "Run like a headless chicken" 3-mi (5 k) race.

Olsen would feed Mike with an eyedropper.

BELIEVE IT OR NOT—By RIPLEY

(Copyright. 1932)

CLINTON W. BLUME
1400 Ocean Parkway, Brooklyn

LOST A SCRUB BRUSH AT SEA, WHEN
ARMY TRANSPORT SANK 500 MILES OFF COAST OF FRANCE,
AND IT WAS WASHED ASHORE AT HIS FEET IN BROOKLYN
ONE YEAR LATER!

6-20-32

Original Ripley cartoon from June 20, 1932.

A Brush with Fate

Robert Ripley always received vast amounts of letters from readers submitting Believe it or Not! stories, but his mailbag really started to bulge after his publisher launched a series of contests offering various prizes to readers who provided the best strange-but-true stories.

Regional newspapers offered $1,000 for the best Believe It or Not! facts, and these successful local contests gave way to the first national Believe It or Not! contest in 1932, which led to Ripley receiving 2.5 million submissions in just two weeks.

The winner of the inaugural contest was Clinton Blume of Brooklyn, whose story was suitably incredible. As his triumphant cartoon of June 20, 1932, explained, Blume had "lost a scrub brush at sea, when an army transport sank 500 mi (800 km) off the coast of France, and it was washed ashore at his feet in Brooklyn one year later!"

Blume's serendipitous tale was supported by photos of him holding the missing scrub bush, helpfully inscribed with his initials.

Blume claimed the generous top prize of a Curtiss-Wright airplane, gifted in person by Robert Ripley himself, complete with a flying course so he could pilot the machine himself. Runners-up prizes included a Studebaker sedan, a television (still a rarity in 1932), a luxury Cuban holiday, and a 24-volume encyclopedia.

Featured in:
- **June 20, 1932 cartoon**
- **2018 anniversary book, *Ripley's Believe It or Not! 100 Years***

25

Featured in:
- 2018 anniversary book *Ripley's Believe It or Not! 100 Years*
- Odditoriums around the world

Strange Mail

In 1929 alone, Robert Ripley received a million letters, breaking all known records for mail received by one person. In a 1936 poll, he was voted the most popular American, beating President Roosevelt, champion boxer Jack Dempsey, and Hollywood actor James Cagney.

Robert Ripley among his piles of fan mail.

Ripley's many followers (or "Rip-O-Maniacs" as some called themselves) obviously thought he was so famous that they could dispense with traditional methods of addressing mail to him. One correspondent simply taped Ripley's photograph to an envelope, pasted on a two-cent stamp, and mailed it with no address. Normally the letter would have been dumped into the dead-letter office, but postal workers knew where to send it, and when news of its successful delivery became public knowledge and a cash prize was given to its author, dozens of imitators tried to go one better.

Letters were sent to Ripley in Confederate Army code or in Boy Scout semaphore. They were written on wood, glass, rocks, bones, and even a grain of rice. One was addressed to "the damnedest liar in the world," while another mailed it to "the person that knows more, tells more, seen more, hears more, draws more 'stranger than fiction' than any person in the world." One of the most ingenious was an envelope with a drawing of a bird in place of an address. When viewed under a magnifying glass, the bird's shape was seen to be made up

of the words "Robert Ripley" repeated thousands of times.

In April 1930, U.S. postmaster general Walter Brown decided that Ripley's fan mail was getting out of hand and ordered that in the future all inadequately addressed mail should be returned to the sender or sent to the dead-letter office. Brown announced: "Postal clerks have had to devote too much time recently to deciphering freak letters intended for Ripley."

In recent years, Ripley's Believe It or Not! has run a Strange Mail contest, where people are encouraged to mail weird objects to the company's Orlando headquarters without any form of packaging. Among items that have been received—some from as far away as Russia and Finland—are a toilet seat, an inflatable monkey, a zucchini, a rubber skeleton, a bowling ball, a meal from McDonald's taped to a plastic plate, and the 2014 winner, a tree stump. Pat Moser, of King, North Carolina, sent the stump—the remains of a tree that had been felled by a storm—and, believe it or not, when he began cutting it up for firewood he discovered a horseshoe embedded inside it!

26

Hot Stepper

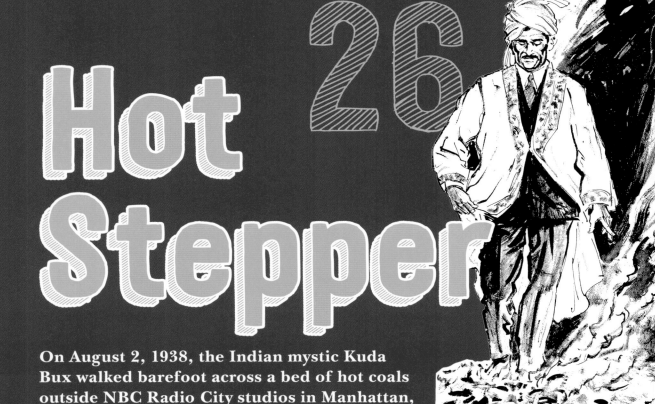

On August 2, 1938, the Indian mystic Kuda Bux walked barefoot across a bed of hot coals outside NBC Radio City studios in Manhattan, New York, for Robert Ripley's radio show.

Featured in:
- The *Ripley's Believe It or Not!* radio program in 1938
- May 2, 1952 cartoon

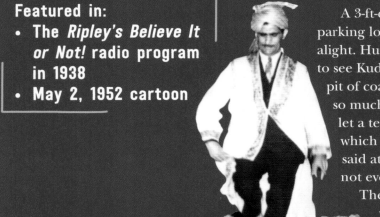

A 3-ft-deep (0.9-m) trench was dug in the parking lot, filled with charcoal logs and set alight. Hundreds of onlookers were present to see Kuda twice dance lightly across the pit of coals before walking away without so much as a limp. He then sat down to let a team of doctors examine his feet, which emerged unscathed. As Ripley said at the time, "the man's feet were not even warm!"

The ability to avoid injury while fire walking seems to stem from the fact that people walk on hot ashes, not on flaming coals, and because the heat vaporizes water in the skin, producing a short-lived, but effective, film to protect the feet.

CHAPTER 2

People

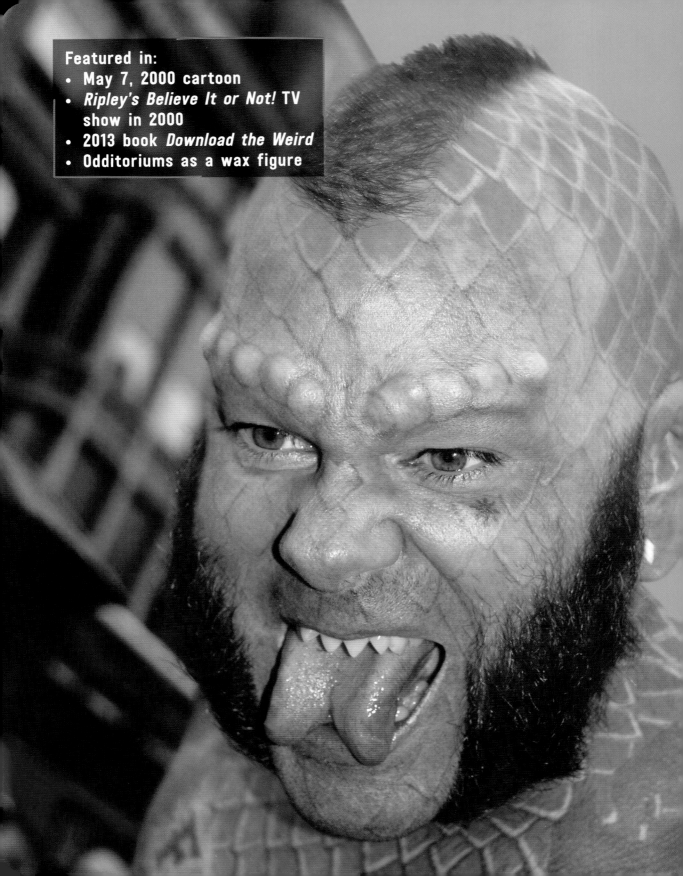

Featured in:
- May 7, 2000 cartoon
- *Ripley's Believe It or Not!* TV show in 2000
- 2013 book *Download the Weird*
- Odditoriums as a wax figure

27

Body Shock

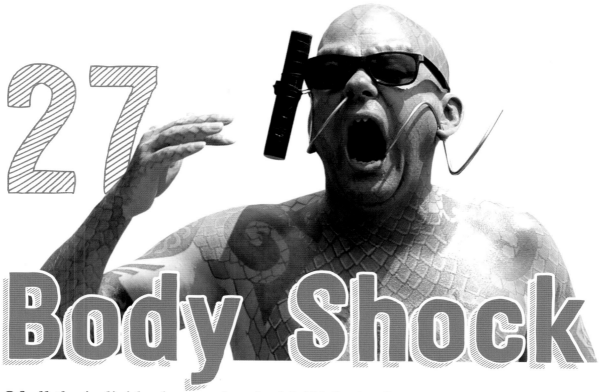

Of all the individuals associated with Ripley's, those mavericks pushing the boundaries of body modification have turned the most heads. They range from the tattooed ladies who broke taboos by displaying their body art in the early 20th century to modern pioneers such as Erik "Lizard Man" Sprague, Eva "Dragon Lady" Medusa, and María José Cristerna, the Vampire Lady of Mexico.

Erik Sprague, a performance artist from Austin, Texas, is one of Ripley's most iconic individuals. He has spent tens of thousands of dollars transforming into a reptile-man hybrid. Sprague's body modifications began with a simple ear piercing at the age of 18, which became the first in a long series of body piercings and tattoos.

Erik has undergone several hundred hours of tattooing since 1994, and is now almost covered in green lizard "scales." He also has stretched ear lobes, a surgically bifurcated tongue—split in two like a lizard's—and his front teeth have been

filed to sharp points, but he can still eat normally. Five Teflon ridges have been implanted into each brow to resemble horns, a painful five-hour operation. Erik has estimated that it would cost in the region of $250,000 to replicate his look, should you be so inclined.

Eva Tiamat Baphomet Medusa, otherwise known as the Dragon Lady, has undergone an extreme body modification in order to transform into a dragon. A former banker now living in Texas, Tiamat has had her nose and ears removed, her tongue split, the whites of her eyes tattooed

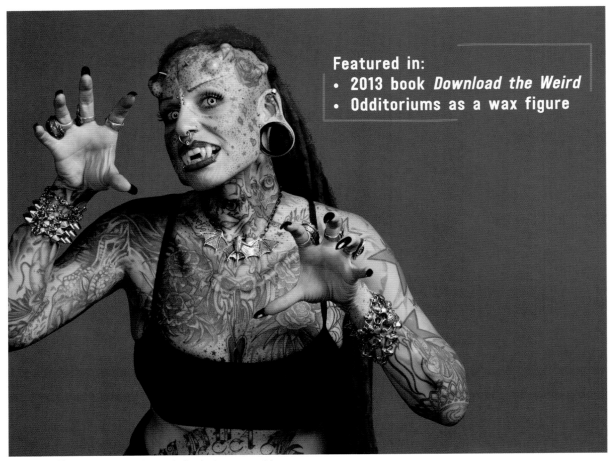

About 95% of Vampire Woman's body is covered in tattoos.

green, horns implanted in her head, and many teeth removed—so that her mouth resembles that of a rattlesnake.

The Dragon Lady also has extensive tattoos that resemble reptilian scales covering her face and body as part of a 25-year, $60,000 ongoing transformation. She claims that after her nose and ears were removed—both of which she has kept as souvenirs—her sense of hearing and smell were both heightened, but she now suffers from a persistent runny rose.

Her nasal modification was inspired by Lord Voldemort, the villain from Harry Potter, but Eva took it further, creating her own unique nose and removing both ears, which she calls "the double Van Gogh,"

referencing the famous artist's self-inflicted injury.

María José Cristerna, a mother of four and former lawyer from Mexico, has had almost 50 body modifications in order to transform herself into the Vampire Woman.

These include many piercings, tattoos covering 95% of her body, large earlobe tunnels, permanent fangs, and transdermal (under the skin) implants on her head, chest, and arms that include horns made from titanium.

Tattoo artist María told Ripley's that her body modification has been an evolving process since she was a teenager, but she reinvented herself as "Vampire Woman" as a sign of strength after troubles in her life.

Featured in:
- 2017 book *Shatter Your Senses!*

28 Colin Furze

YouTuber and ingenious inventor Colin Furze, from Lincolnshire, England, has created some of the wackiest machines and vehicles ever conceived. The former plumber has fitted a baby stroller with a motorcycle engine, enabling it to reach speeds of 50 mph (80 kmph), and designed a fairground bumper car that can travel 20 times faster than its regular speed.

He has also built a 72-ft-long (22-m) motorcycle that can seat 23 people, yet still reach speeds of 35 mph (56 kmph). Furze, whose YouTube channel has 6.6 million subscribers and more than 700 million views, has also created superhero-like magnetic shoes that enable the wearer to walk on the ceiling.

In 2014, Furze built a 16-ft-high (5-m) "fart machine," which consisted of a giant pulse jet engine housed in a pair of specially constructed buttocks. He transported it to Kent and aimed it at France to see whether it could be heard 21 mi (33 km) away across the English Channel. People in France reported hearing a "faint rumble."

Taking the temperature down a little was an ice bike—a somewhat-rideable bicycle fitted with wheels entirely made of ice. One of Furze's most remarkable achievements was building a working hover bike powered by two giant gas-powered fans originally designed for paragliding.

In 2016, the master-maker built an 18-ft-tall (5.5-m) recreation of an AT-ACT walker from *Rogue One: A Star Wars Story*. Furze built it for his friend's son in six weeks, using materials such as wooden panels and Chinese woks. The head can move and a ladder drops from inside, revealing a playroom full of Star Wars-themed gadgets and toys.

More recently he teamed up with fellow YouTuber James Brunton to build a

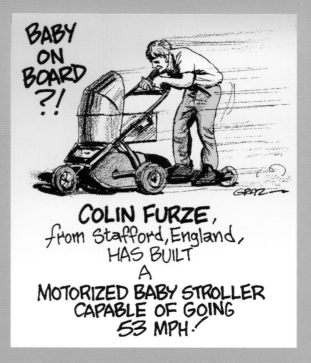

BABY ON BOARD ?!

COLIN FURZE, from Stafford, England, HAS BUILT A MOTORIZED BABY STROLLER CAPABLE OF GOING 53 MPH!

10-ft-tall (3-m) recreation of the Hulkbuster Iron Man suit to celebrate the release of *Avengers: Infinity War*. The robot can punch and throw flames from its palms!

A 23-seater motorcycle that can reach speeds of up to 35 mph (56 kmph)!

29 Disk Wearers

Featured in:
- Various cartoons throughout the years
- The first *Ripley's Believe It or Not!* book in 1929
- *Ripley's Believe It or Not!* TV show in 2001
- 2004 *Ripley's Believe It or Not!* book
- Odditoriums as a wax figure

The "labret" body modification is characterized by large discs inserted into stretched holes in the upper or lower lips.

The practice is less popular than it used to be, but it still continues today among indigenous tribes in Africa and South America. Girls of the Mursi tribe from Ethiopia have cuts made in their lower lips when they are teenagers, if they are willing, and a small disc of clay or wood is inserted. Over time larger plates are inserted so that the lip stretches, sometimes to an incredible degree.

Among the Sara people of Chad, discs may be placed in both lips. In South America, it is native men rather than women that traditionally wear lip plates, such as those displayed by elder members of the Kayapo in Brazil.

The largest known lip disk measured 7.7 in (19.5 cm) in diameter and was worn by Ataye Eligidagne of Ethiopia in 2014. The reasons behind the tradition are not entirely understood, but it is thought to be a sign of coming of age.

In the 1930s, after appearing in the Paris Colonial Exposition, lip-disc-wearing members of the Sara tribe were brought to America to appear in sideshows in the famous Ringling Bros. and Barnum & Bailey circuses. They were cast as "Crocodile Lipped women," or the Ubangis, a made-up name that sounded suitably exotic but has often been used since to describe women who wear lip plates.

Original Ripley cartoon from July 27, 1924.

30 Harlem Hoarders

In March 1947, the New York City police received an anonymous tip about a dead body in the crumbling mansion at 2807 Fifth Avenue, Manhattan. The house belonged to brothers Langley and Homer Collyer. When the police arrived, they found the body of Homer—but that was only after five hours of searching through literal tons of junk. Langley was still missing.

Upon arrival, the police broke down the door and were confronted by an impenetrable wall of junk piled to the ceiling. The lower windows were barred, so they burrowed in through a second-floor window. After a two-week search of the dilapidated house, Langley's corpse was finally discovered. He had been crushed by his own trash in a tunnel of garbage, just 10 ft (3 m) from where his brother was found.

When both their parents died in the 1920s, Homer and Langley remained in the five-story family house. In 1933 Homer suffered a stroke, losing his sight and becoming paralyzed. He would never leave the house again, and Langley became his caretaker. Eventually he too barely showed himself in daylight, only leaving the house for food and newspapers that he said were for Homer's benefit, should his sight return.

As the neighborhood began to change from the upper class "Millionaire's Avenue," the brothers grew paranoid and Langley began collecting junk with which to fortify their mansion. He moved through the building in an elaborate maze of tunnels burrowed through the piles of debris. Fearful of burglars, he set up several trash traps designed to collapse piles of heavy junk onto unsuspecting intruders. His obsession with security, however, would be the death of him.

There were more than 120 tons of junk in the Collyer house.

After searching for two weeks, Langley's body was found just 10 ft (3 m) away from his brother.

Police and city workers removed more than 120 tons of largely worthless ephemera from the house before they found Langley. This included thousands of newspapers dating back to the First World War, 20,000 books, firearms, several grand pianos, and other instruments, including antique violins—not to mention multiple bicycles, tree trunks, various medical machinery, and a Ford Model T automobile in pieces in the basement.

The police investigation determined that Langley had been taking Homer a sandwich through a narrow tunnel of trash when he triggered one of his own booby-traps. He was pinned to the floor by a heavy suitcase and bundles of newspapers. Lost in his own labyrinth, he had either starved or

suffocated. A frail Homer had succumbed not long afterward.

Today the Collyer legend still lives on in New York. Although the house was demolished not long after their deaths, the vacant plot was turned into Collyer Brothers Park in the 1960s. Among modern firefighters, a "Collyer Mansion" is a home filled with so much junk that it poses a danger to its occupants.

Featured in:
- *Ripley's Believe It or Not!* Special Edition 2005 book
- 2018 BION Brief video and blog post

Featured in:
- September 26, 1974 cartoon
- 2017 episode of YouTube show
  Cool Stuff Strange Things

31

A newsman photographs the crate in which Spiers shipped himself across the globe.

Man in a Box

Reg Spiers successfully shipped himself as air cargo from the U.K. all the way to Australia! The 22-year-old javelin thrower wanted to compete at the 1964 Tokyo Olympics, but had not thrown the qualifying distance in his home country of Australia. He traveled to the U.K. to try and reach the Olympic standard, but ended up injuring his elbow and having his wallet stolen.

Finding himself with no Olympic entry, no money for a plane ticket, and keen to get to back to Australia in time for his daughter's birthday, Spiers hatched a cunning plan to get himself home. He would travel to Australia hidden in a crate and loaded into a plane's cargo hold.

Spiers had been working in the cargo section at London Heathrow airport, where he had noticed animals coming into the country on a "cash on delivery" basis. "If they can do it, I can do it," he thought.

With the help of U.K. javelin thrower John McSorley, Spiers built a box measuring 5 ft (1.5 m) long, 3 ft (1 m) deep, and 2.5 ft (0.75 m) wide, which he described as "surprisingly comfortable." The box was fitted with straps for the athlete to brace himself as the crate was hauled around.

Spiers labeled the cargo "synthetic polymer emulsion," and invented a chemical company from which to send the package. He addressed the crate to a shoe company in Perth, Australia. Spiers climbed inside the crate with the help of his friend, who nailed it shut. His supplies consisted of a couple of tins of peaches and a bottle of water.

REGINALD SPIERS of Adelaide, Australia, BROKE, AFTER FAILING TO QUALIFY IN THE JAVELIN EVENTS IN THE OLYMPIC TRYOUTS IN LONDON, ENG. (1964), HAD A FRIEND SHIP HIM HOME BY PLANE, C.O.D., IN A PACKING CRATE

McSorley drove him to Heathrow Airport and loaded him onto an Air India Boeing 707 bound for Australia via Paris and Bombay—a 13,000 mi (20,900 km) flight. Spiers had to wait in the crate for 24 hours before the plane even took off due to fog. Several hours later the plane reached Bombay, where he had to endure another tortuous delay on the hot tarmac. The athlete later said that while he never got hungry during the 63-hour flight, he was "mighty thirsty" once his water ran out.

When the plane eventually touched down in Australia, Spiers waited for another nine hours in the customs shed until he dared to get out of the box. He stole a quick beer from a pallet, put on a suit he had with him, then hitchhiked all the way back to Adelaide—a 1,700-mi (2,700 km) journey in itself.

Meanwhile, back in the U.K., Spiers's accomplice John McSorley had not heard a word from the intrepid traveler, and he feared the worst. He contacted a newspaper in order to get the word out, and Spiers became a media sensation. Customs officials questioned him about his exploits, but no further action was taken, and he didn't even have to pay the cargo fee. He went on to win Australian javelin titles in 1967 and 1977.

32
Mr. Eats Everything

Featured in:
- 1990 and 2016 cartoons
- 2004 *Ripley's Believe It or Not!* book
- 2009 book *Twists: Human Body*

Ripley's has featured many fearless feeders with strong stomachs, including competitive speed-eaters, but none of them had an appetite like Michel Lotito.

Known as "Monsieur Mangetout," meaning "Mr. Eats Everything," Lotito is famous for munching his way through objects that no other person would describe as fit for consumption. The Frenchman had pica, a condition that causes sufferers to crave inedible objects such as dirt, rocks, and metal.

When he was hungry, which was most of the time, Lotito would eat around 2 lb (1 kg) of metal a day, eventually working his way through 18 bicycles, several shopping carts, televisions, one coffin, and chunks of iron from the Eiffel Tower.

Monsieur Mangetout would wash down the metal with mineral oil to ease its "passage" through his body, and was also partial to nails and light bulbs.

He is most famous, however, for something that really shouldn't be possible— he ate an airplane. Between 1978 and 1980 Lotito devoured an entire Cessna 150. Doctors who studied his digestive system discovered that his stomach lining was unusually thick, which helped to ensure that his favorite spiky snacks didn't cause a fatal perforation.

Despite having the world's weirdest diet, Lotito once said that he was unable to eat bananas and boiled eggs because they made him ill. In 2007 Lotito passed away at the age of 57, but although he had eaten an estimated 18,000 lb (8,160 kg) of metal over the years, he died from natural causes.

33

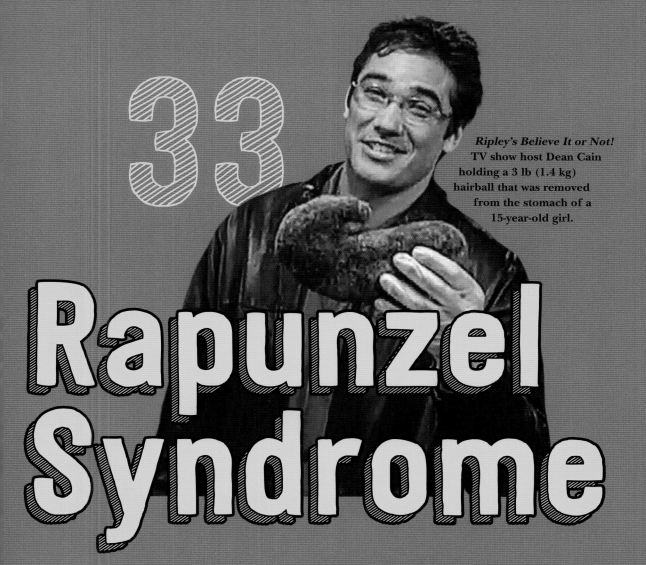

Ripley's Believe It or Not! TV show host Dean Cain holding a 3 lb (1.4 kg) hairball that was removed from the stomach of a 15-year-old girl.

Rapunzel Syndrome

Trichophagia is a rare psychological condition that causes sufferers to compulsively eat their own hair.

Trichophagia is linked to trichotillomania, a disorder usually affecting girls who feel compelled to pull their own hair out. A portion of these sufferers also eat their hair, which can lead to serious medical complications.

Human hair is not broken down by the stomach, meaning that if enough hair is ingested it can cause a hairball, or "trichobezoar," to build up in the sufferer's

Featured in:
- *Ripley's Believe It or Not!* TV show in 2000
- **Various cartoons and books over the years**

guts, causing ulcers or serious blockages. Cases are rare, but they can be fatal without surgical intervention. Such cases are also known as "Rapunzel syndrome," after the long-haired fairy tale princess.

Featured in:
- February 4, 1930 cartoon
- 2011 book *Strikingly True*
- 2018 *Ripley's Believe It or Not!* comic Issue 1

34

Phineas Gage

Phineas Gage survived what should have been a fatal injury when an iron rod blasted through his face and out of the top of his head. Instead, he became one of the most remarkable stories in medical history and one of the first cases to show a link between personality change and brain trauma.

Gage was a foreman for a railroad company in Vermont who blasted rocks to clear space for the tracks to be laid. One day in September 1848, the 25-year-old was preparing a detonation, packing gunpowder into holes in the rock using a 43 in (110 cm) iron tamping rod. Usually Gage would wait for his assistant to lay sand over the explosives before he used the rod, but this time he didn't, and as he struck with the metal bar, the powder ignited. Instead of cracking the rock, the explosion propelled the 13 lb (6 kg) iron rod right through Gage's face and out of the top of his head with such force that it landed 30 ft (10 m) away, covered with "blood and brain." It should surely have been a fatal injury, but instead the incident began one of the most remarkable stories in medical history.

Gage was not dead—indeed, he may not have even lost consciousness—and he was able to walk away from the scene while talking to his co-workers. He spat out "about half a teacupful" of his brain matter as a doctor examined him, but was still able to tell the physician, "Here is business enough for you." Gage lost consciousness after his wound became infected, but after several months he had made a miraculous recovery. All motor functions were intact, but he was blind in the left eye, which the rod damaged on its way through his skull.

Gage's case became famous; he was even photographed with the offending iron rod, his left eye closed but with no other visible sign of injury. Although Gage was physically able—he lived for 12 years after the accident—mentally he was not the same, or in his doctor's words, "no longer Gage," and friends reported that post-explosion Gage was irritable, angry, and untrustworthy, to the extent that he was unable to return to his old job. His memory and intelligence were the same as before, but he had lost his inhibitions, and his ability to function in civilized society, impulsively indulging in the "grossest profanity."

After failing to find work on the railroads, Gage made public appearances with the offending tamping iron, even being paraded at P.T. Barnum's famous American Museum in New York City. He traveled to Chile to find a job on stagecoaches, and eventually returned home to work on the family farm, where he died in 1860, aged 36. He had been suffering seizures likely linked to his brain damage.

Doctors would study the injury for many years; Gage's case gave a valuable early insight into how the brain could function after serious injury, and how brain damage in different areas of the organ could affect behavior. Gage's story made such an impact on medical study that his skull—with a large hole clearly visible—and the iron rod can today be seen in the Harvard Medical School museum.

THE MOST AMAZING ACCIDENT THAT EVER HAPPENED!

A CROW BAR 4 feet long - weighing 14 lbs. WAS DRIVEN COMPLETELY THROUGH THE HEAD OF Phineas P. Gage — AND HE LIVED 13 YEARS LONGER! — Dying a natural death

SMILES SMILES IS THE LONGEST WORD IN THE ENGLISH LANGUAGE There is a MILE between the first and last letters

HIS SKULL AND CROW BAR ARE ON

Original Ripley cartoon from February 4, 1930.

35
Feeling
Blue

When someone tells you they're blue, you know they mean that they are feeling down about something. But for a handful of people throughout history, and even up to modern times, being blue was quite literal.

Suffering from stress-related dermatitis after his father's death, Paul Karason of Madera, California, decided to treat it with his own mixture of colloidal silver, a medicine widely used before the discovery of penicillin. However, silver has been banned in U.S. medicines since 1999 because it causes argyria, a condition that turns the skin blue. He probably exacerbated the problem by rubbing the silver into the peeling skin on his face as well as taking it orally. Karason died of a stroke unrelated to his argyria in 2013 at the age of 62.

While Karason's blue façade was the result of self-prescribed silver, blue skin can also appear naturally. Just ask the Fugate family—also known as the blue people of Kentucky. In 1820, blue-skinned Martin Fugate married Elizabeth Smith in the remote settlement Troublesome Creek, Kentucky.

Smith was described as being red-haired and as pale "as the mountain laurel that blooms every spring around the creek hollows." Unbeknownst to her, she carried the recessive gene for the same blood disorder that made her husband blue— methemoglobinemia.

The combination of genes and a history of inbreeding due to the isolated nature of Troublesome Creek led to generations of a family filled with blue people. When the legend of the blue people had faded into history, it was once again brought to light when a descendent born in 1975 came out with dark blue skin!

Doctors were shocked over Benjamin "Benjy" Stacy's alarming color, but his grandmother and father explained to them that Benjy's great-grandmother was a blue Fugate, making him the great-great-great-great-grandson of Martin Fugate and Elizabeth Smith. Lucky for him, he eventually outgrew his blue hue.

Featured in:
- **January 8, 2006 cartoon**
- **September 11, 2016 cartoon**

THE
HANGING HINDU
An Ascetic performing Gharak Puja.
SUSPENDED FROM A TREE
ON A HOOK FASTENED IN
HIS FLESH.
They hang this way for days.

**Original Ripley cartoon
from May 16, 1923.**

Rip' BENGAL-INDIA

Featured in:
- **Episode** *of Ripley's Believe It
  or Not!* **TV show in 2000**
- **Various cartoons and books
  throughout the years**

36
Suspension Club

Body suspension is a subculture in the world of body modification.
Enthusiasts suspend themselves from hooks pierced through the skin on
various parts of their body and literally hang out, enjoying the sensation.
A "suspension artist" is an expert who will oversee the procedure and
ensure its safety—up to a point! Some more extreme suspension artists
use the hooks to perform incredible feats of strength.

The practice dates back thousands of years to ancient Asia, and was originally linked to religious self-punishment. At modern-day Hindu Tamil festivals in Malaysia, Sri Lanka, and Thailand, the religious roots of body suspension can still be seen. At the Thaipusam festival, which attracts hundreds of thousands of devotees, believers hang items from hooks through their skin, or even pull vehicles with them. Others might pierce their cheeks with kebab skewers.

The Okipa ceremony of the Manda Native American tribe is another example of traditional body suspension. At the climax of the ritual, young men of the tribe, who had fasted and stayed awake for three days already, would be hung aloft from ropes attached to wood spikes pierced through their torso. Buffalo skulls were

A still from the Suspension Club event filmed for the *Ripley's Believe It or Not!* TV show.

Traditional body suspension ceremony performed by the Manda tribe of North America.

hung from cuts made in their legs. When they fainted, the ordeal was over.

Featured in the first episode of the 2000 revival of the *Ripley's Believe It or Not!* TV show was the Suspension Club of Dallas, Texas. With meat hooks attached to their backs, nine members dangled from a giant crane in front of the St. Augustine, Florida, Odditorium.

Featured in:
- December 6, 1940 radio broadcast
- February 16, 1941 cartoon

Widdecombe and Tapscott reenacting their ordeal at sea.

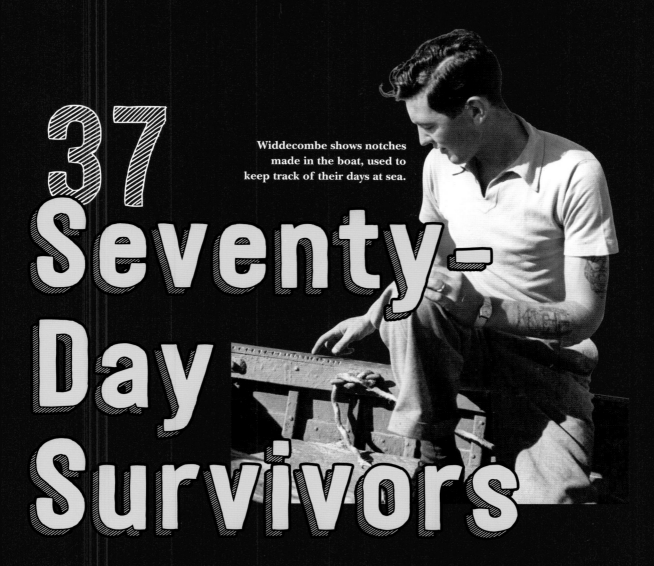

37 Seventy-Day Survivors

Widdecombe shows notches made in the boat, used to keep track of their days at sea.

On the December 6, 1940, broadcast of his radio program, Robert Ripley interviewed Roy Widdicombe and Robert Tapscott, two British sailors who had survived 70 days on the Atlantic Ocean after Germans sank their ship, eventually landing in the Bahamas.

The broadcast also featured the Duke of Windsor, Governor of the Bahamas, and formerly King Edward VIII, who read a statement about their journey—the first time a member of the British royal family had appeared on commercial radio. The Duke and Duchess had previously met the sailors in the hospital in Nassau.

Welsh merchant seamen Widdicombe and Tapscott were onboard the coal-carrying ship SS *Anglo-Saxon* on a voyage from Wales to Argentina, when on the night of August 21, 1940, she came under attack from the German cruiser *Widder*. After heavy shelling caused explosions on board, killing many of the crew, the

Widder fired a torpedo, and *Anglo-Saxon* sank within an hour, hundreds of miles from land.

The German guns had damaged the ship's lifeboats, and those that did manage to launch were gunned down in the water. Tapscott, Widdicombe, and five others managed to escape the sinking vessel in an 18-ft (5.5-m) "jolly boat." They floated past the Germans in the dark and then started to row. They had some water, tinned meat, and biscuits on board, but it would not be enough to keep them all alive.

Of the seven who escaped the sinking, only Tapscott and Widdicombe survived the trip. The others succumbed to either injuries sustained in the attack or dehydration and malnutrition leading to delirium and desperation; some slipped into the water on purpose.

Ripley posing with the two survivors.

Tapscott and Widdicombe both considered giving up, but they held on long enough for a rainstorm that gave them precious drinking water. A flying fish that landed in the boat sustained them briefly, along with small crabs, but they grew so hungry that they ate their skin as it peeled, and even their own shoes.

They survived mid-Atlantic storms and hitting a whale. After 60 days at sea, they were too weak to stand, let alone row, and each lost up to 80 lb (36 kg) in weight. On October 30, 1940, the jolly boat finally washed up in the Bahamas, where it was discovered by a farmer, 70 days after the sinking of SS *Anglo-Saxon*.

In January 1941, Widdicombe was well enough to return home, and boarded another cargo ship returning to Britain. Perhaps he had used up all his luck on the jolly boat voyage: the ship was sunk by a German U-boat off the coast of Scotland, and this time there were no survivors.

Tapscott later rejoined the war effort and returned to Wales where he married and had a daughter. Twenty years after the sinking of the *Anglo-Saxon*, he committed suicide, unable to deal with the impact of the terrible voyage.

Original Ripley cartoon from February 16, 1941.

One of the wax
figures of Walter
that can be seen at
Ripley's Odditoriums
around the world.

38 Weighty Walter

Featured in:
- 2015 book *Eye-Popping Oddities*
- Odditoriums as a wax figure

Ripley's Believe It or Not! has long featured some of the most remarkable physical specimens on the planet, and Walter Hudson of Hempstead, New York, one of the largest men ever to have lived, was certainly remarkable. In 1987 at the age of 42, he was heavier than a small horse, weighing at least 1,200 lb (544 kg)—easily the biggest man on Earth. Ripley's has immortalized Hudson in life-sized wax figures on display in several Ripley's Odditoriums.

Walter's insatiable appetite meant that as a six-year-old he had already ballooned to a weight of 125 lb (57 kg). At 15 years old, he weighed as much as two grown men and rarely left his house. By the 1980s, his waist was 103 in (261 cm) in circumference, and at 55 in (140 cm), his legs were far wider than most people's waists.

Hudson's enormous weight was supported by superhuman feats of eating. It's estimated that he would regularly consume 20,000 calories a day—twice as much as an Olympic swimmer, and more than the suggested weekly intake for a regular person. Walter's daily diet would typically consist of a dozen sausages, eight portions of fries, two chickens, 20 cupcakes, 1.5 gal (6 l) of soda, a dozen eggs, 1 lb (454 g) of bacon, one loaf of bread, and eight cheeseburgers.

Hudson spent almost all of his time in bed and could not stand without help, which made calculating his exact weight extremely difficult. In 1987, an attempt was made to weigh him on an industrial scale, with a group of local weightlifters enlisted

Christmas 1987: Walter left his room for the first time in 16 years.

as support. His size meant that he wore only a bed sheet, as he couldn't find clothes to fit his gigantic frame. The scales displayed their maximum—1,000 lb (454 kg)—and then broke.

Around this time, Walter did start to slim down. On Christmas in 1987 Walter made his way from his bedroom to his living room for the first time in 16 years. By mid-1988 Walter had lost at least 600 lb (272 kg), taking the first steps outside his home in 18 years at a relatively svelte 520 lb (236 kg). He even founded a clothing line for plus-size fashions. Unfortunately, the weight loss didn't last, and Hudson died of a heart attack on December 24, 1991, at age 46. He weighed 1,125 lb (510 kg). Walter was buried in a 4-ft-6-in-wide (1.4-m) casket made from 800 lb (363 kg) of reinforced steel. It required a crane to maneuver.

Walter's casket was 4.5 ft (1.4 m) wide and required a crane to move.

The
PRIZE-
WINNING
CARTOON
of 1939

STABBED TO DEATH BY A BASEBALL!

Original Ripley cartoon from January 17, 1940.

39 Foul Ball

On October 25, 1902, Stanton Walker was watching a baseball game at Morristown, Ohio, sitting between two companions, Leroy Wilson and Frank Hyde, who was keeping score. Hyde asked Wilson for a knife with which to sharpen his pencil. As the pocketknife was handed to Walker to pass on, his hand was struck by a foul ball, and the blade was driven into his heart—killing him.

Robert Ripley featured the story in the cartoon in 1939, and again in January 1940, when it was declared the "prize-winning cartoon of 1939," submitted by a Mr. Ambrose Flanagan of Syracuse, Ohio, who also won the honor of being illustrated by Ripley.

Featured in:
- 1939 and 1940 cartoons
- 1983 book *Ripley's Believe It or Not! Book of Chance*
- 2008 book *Ripley's Believe It or Not! Baseball Oddities & Trivia*

AIN'T HE PURDY?

WHAT WAS THOUGHT TO BE A WAX FIGURE OF A HANGED MAN IN A FUNHOUSE TURNED OUT TO BE **THE PRESERVED BODY** OF *ELMER McCURDY* WHO WAS KILLED IN A 1911 SHOOTOUT!

WORKMEN AT THE PIKE AMUSEMENT PARK DISCOVERED THE TRUTH IN THE 1970'S WHEN THEY ATTEMPTED TO REATTACH AN ARM THAT HAD BROKEN OFF — **AND FOUND A BONE!**

GRAZIANO

40
Elmer McCurdy

Inept at robbing trains, Oklahoma outlaw Elmer McCurdy made more in death than he ever did while he was alive. He was killed in a 1911 gunfight, his last words being the familiar "You'll never take me alive"—but it was then that his corpse took on a life of its own.

When nobody came forward to claim the body, the mortician used him as a promotional tool to demonstrate his skills. He embalmed Elmer with preservative chemicals and exhibited him as "The Bandit Who Wouldn't Give Up," inviting customers to insert a nickel in McCurdy's mouth.

The attraction proved so profitable that numerous carnival operators put in bids for the mummified outlaw, but the undertaker resisted all offers until being duped by a man claiming to be McCurdy's long-lost brother. Led to believe that McCurdy was to be given a proper burial, the undertaker handed him over, only to see him exhibited by a traveling carnival two weeks later.

For the next 60 years, Elmer pursued a posthumous career in show business. His body was sold on to various wax museums and carnivals, although one haunted house proprietor in South Dakota turned it down because he did not think it was sufficiently lifelike.

In 1976, the TV show *The Six Million Dollar Man* was filming at The Pike, a California amusement park. A crew member bumped into a body wrapped up like a mummy hanging above him. The rope holding the figure broke and fell on the boy, knocking him to the floor, and one of its arms snapped off.

To their horror, the crew realized it was not a prop, but a real human body, and a real Halloween horror. They had found Elmer McCurdy.

Elmer was finally returned to Oklahoma and given a proper burial in 1977—66 years after his death. The state medical examiner ordered that his casket be encased in concrete so that his restless corpse would never be disturbed again.

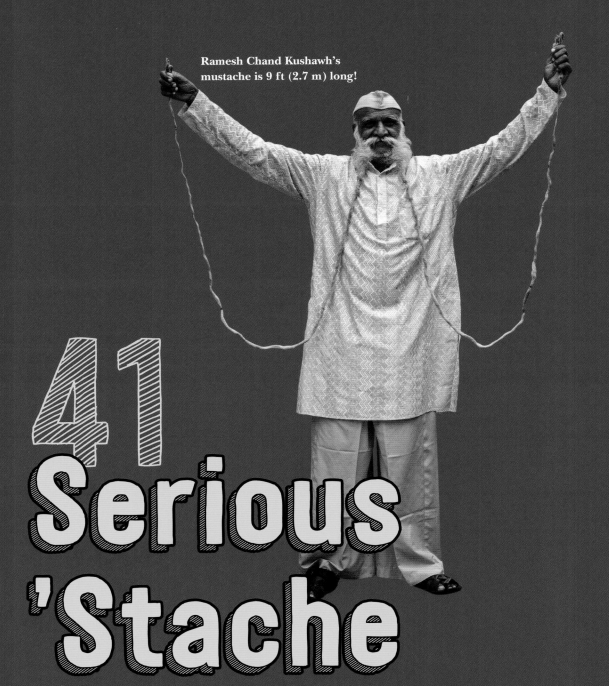

Ramesh Chand Kushawh's mustache is 9 ft (2.7 m) long!

41
Serious 'Stache

In 1933 Robert Ripley invited an Indian policeman, Desar Arjan Dangar, to appear at the first Believe It or Not! Odditorium at the Chicago World's Fair. Dangar's unbelievable attribute was an 8.6-ft-long (2.6-m) mustache, which he had cultivated for many years.

The GREAT MUSTACHE
8 FEET 8 INCHES WIDE!

Lesur Arjan Dangar — of Kathiawar, India.

Unfortunately, Dangar never made it on stage, as his facial hair suffered an injury. The policeman was angry when he realized that his agent was keeping most of his appearance fee, and in the ensuing scuffle he lost one half of his magnificent mustache.

Recently Ripley's heard of another Indian man who is following his countryman's hirsute heroics. For the past 25 years, 78-year-old Ramesh Chand Kushawh, of Uttar Pradesh, has grown his mustache to an astonishing 9 ft (2.7 m). He keeps his facial hair safely coiled in a ball on his head and refuses to see his daughter or grandchildren, for fear that they'd damage it.

He says he keeps the hair healthy by washing it in milk and applying curd and cream every day. The longest mustache on record belonged to Ram Singh Chauhan, also of India. In 2010 his world-beating whiskers measured 14 ft (4.29 m).

Featured in:
- September 24, 1933 cartoon
- 2018 book *A Century of Strange!*

Many police departments throughout India offer bonuses and prizes for officers that grow mustaches.

Featured in:
- The *Ripley's Believe It or Not!* Vitaphone show

42

Horned People

In one of Ripley's early Vitaphone shows, he told his viewers about a man he met in Africa who had two 8-in-long (20-cm) horns on his head. Ripley said, "I met him myself. He told me he shed them like a deer sheds his antlers every year... He is without a doubt the strangest man I've ever seen."

For centuries, people with "horns" have been a subject of fascination. Doctors believe that growths such as these are a form of hyperplasia, an excess of normal body tissue. They can be caused by tumors, which are usually benign, or skin damage caused by sun exposure or burns.

In 1922 Ripley drew a portrait of Francis Trovillon, "The Horned Man of Mezieres," who lived in France in the 16th century. According to historical accounts, Trovillon's head began to swell when he was a child, and by the time he was a teenager, the growth was as big as a man's finger. By the age of 30 he had the equivalent of a ram's horn on his head, and he was exhibited in Paris and Orleans.

In the 1930s Robert Ripley encountered something similar while visiting northeastern China. Wang, a farmer from Manchukuo, had a 14 in (36 cm) horn growing from the back of his head. Today "The Human Unicorn" can be seen as a lifelike wax figure at Ripley's Odditoriums. Believe it or not, these would not be the last horned people featured by Ripley's!

In 1991 kung fu practitioner Wang Ying, from Jiangsu, China, discovered a tumor the size of a grain of rice on his forehead. Fourteen years later, the swelling had grown to almost 2 in (5 cm) in length and 1 in (3 cm) in diameter. When doctors told Wang that they couldn't operate on the tumor because of its location, 74-year-old Wang Ying decided to incorporate it into his strongman act. He would lift bricks tied to a length of rope looped around the protruding facial growth.

In 2011, a Chinese woman from Henan, China, sought treatment at Beijing Military General Hospital for a mysterious horn growing on the left side of her head. Despite having a small growth removed from her forehead in 2008, the object grew again in the same position and had reached a size of almost 8 in (20 cm) when surgeons successfully removed it.

Featured in:
- **May 11, 1930 cartoon**
- **Odditoriums as a wax figure**

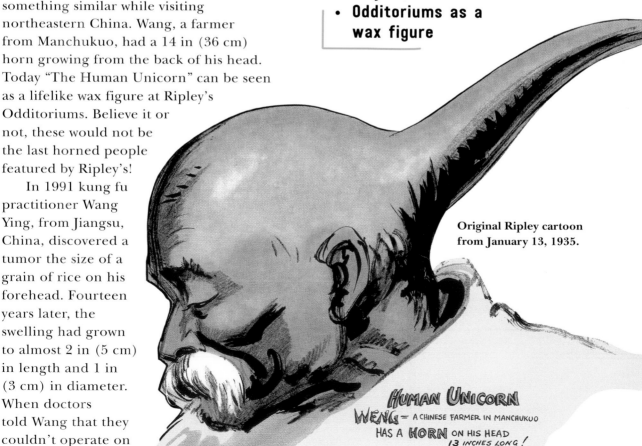

Original Ripley cartoon from January 13, 1935.

HUMAN UNICORN
WENG = A CHINESE FARMER IN MANCHUKUO
HAS A HORN ON HIS HEAD
13 INCHES LONG !

43

The Great Blondin

On June 30, 1859, thousands of people thronged the banks of the Niagara Gorge to watch agog as the greatest stuntman in the world, Charles Blondin, walked 1,300 ft (396 m) across the Niagara River on a tightrope only 2 in (5 cm) thick.

Blondin had only a 26-ft (8-m) long balancing pole for assistance; there was no safety line or net to catch him if he fell 175 ft (53 m) into the swirling waters below. The crowd, who had each paid 50 cents for the spectacle, gasped as he stooped in the middle to haul up a bottle of wine from a boat far below, take a glug, and then continue to the other side.

But the Great Blondin wasn't finished; he completed the return journey back across the river, this time carrying a camera and stopping to take a picture of his audience en route.

Charles Blondin was born Jean-François Gravelet in 1824 in Pas-de-Calais, France. His father was a tightrope walker himself, as was his father before him, and as a young boy he attended a gymnastics school. Gravelet named himself Blondin after the first circus in which he performed. It's thought that by the end of his career Blondin had covered 10,000 mi (16,000 km) on perilous tightropes around the world. He never used a safety line and never relied on a net—he thought to do so would be to tempt fate. His only concessions to safety were guy ropes to prevent the main tightrope from swinging around too much in the wind.

When Blondin announced his Niagara stunt, nobody expected him to actually complete the walk. After the Frenchman successfully defied death not once but twice, he made headlines on both sides of the

on his back, taking 40 minutes to complete the walk. In 1860 he pushed a man across the river in a wheelbarrow. Once safely on the other side, Blondin asked for more volunteers. Watching in the crowd was the Prince of Wales, the future King Edward VII of England, and Blondin offered to take him on the return journey. The prince agreed, but his staff would not allow him to take the trip, so Blondin left the wheelbarrow behind and teetered back across on stilts.

On one occasion he carried a table and chairs onto the rope, then sat down to enjoy a meal and bottle of wine. He went further still when he carried an iron stove across the rope on his back, stopping in the middle to make an omelet. He then lowered the dish to spectators on a boat below.

After Blondin's Niagara heroics made his name, the daredevil took his show on tours of Europe, India, China, South America, and Australia, continuing to perform into his seventies. He died in London in 1897 at the age of 75.

Blondin enjoying a meal and wine halfway down the rope.

Atlantic. When he returned to Niagara Falls that summer to repeat his seminal stunt, more than 20,000 people traveled by train and steamer ship to witness it.

Blondin returned to Niagara on several more occasions. On each walk the master strove to eclipse his previous walks, upping the ante by completing the walk backward, hanging from the tightrope with his hands, dressing up as a gorilla, wearing a sack over his head, being locked in manacles like a prisoner, performing backward somersaults, and balancing on his head for minutes at a time.

In September 1859, Blondin carried his manager, Harry Colcord, across Niagara Falls

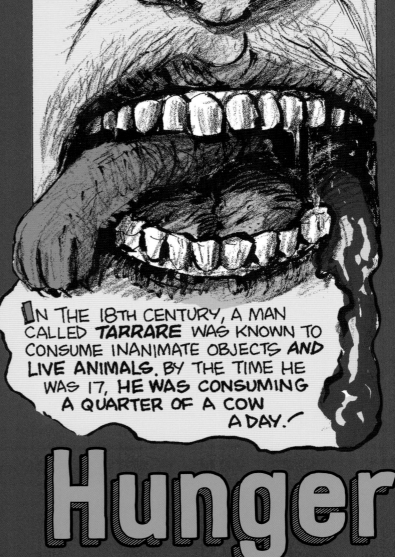

IN THE 18TH CENTURY, A MAN CALLED **TARRARE** WAS KNOWN TO CONSUME INANIMATE OBJECTS **AND** LIVE ANIMALS. BY THE TIME HE WAS 17, HE WAS CONSUMING A QUARTER OF A COW A DAY.

44 The Hunger of Tarrare

Tarrare was an 18th-century Frenchman who became famous for his insatiable appetite. Born in Lyon, he was a slight man who weighed not much more than 100 lb (45 kg), and despite eating vast amounts, he never put on weight.

He became a traveling showman who would entertain audiences by swallowing corks, stones, live animals—including snakes, which was said to have been his favorite—and vast amounts of regular food. He did not fill his stomach in this manner simply for fun or for profit, however; he really did have a hunger that could not be satisfied. He would hang around butcher's shops, waiting to scavenge on the scraps, and he was once witnessed eating 30 lbs (13.6 kg) of raw liver and lungs.

When he joined the French Revolutionary Army, the meager military rations drove him crazy with hunger, and he would eat anything he could find, performing chores for his colleagues so that they left him their rations. But that was not enough, and he was reduced to scavenging through heaps of trash for scraps.

Eventually his inability to feel full led to his admittance to the hospital with exhaustion. During his time in the military medical facility, he came to the notice of doctors who subjected him to various tests to get to the bottom of his bottomless appetite.

During these bizarre experiments, Tarrare consumed 15 portions of food in one sitting, and would swallow eels in one gulp. It's said that in the grip of a crazed hunger, Tarrare seized a live cat, tore out its guts with his teeth, drank its blood, and then ate it, before spitting out the fur, all in front of a doctor.

Despite his bizarre diet, Tarrare bore no outward visual signs of his gruesome gluttony, but it was reported that he smelled so badly that after a particularly heavy meal nobody would go within 20 paces of him.

Featured in
• **June 17, 2017 cartoon**

A French army surgeon had heard of Tarrare's unusual abilities, and put him to work as an unconventional courier. He gave him a box to swallow containing a secret message for a captured French soldier, meaning it could not be intercepted, and he was sent out behind enemy lines. The box was to be retrieved once it had passed through his system. Unfortunately, Tarrare lacked a talent for espionage, and he was captured by enemy forces, beaten, and imprisoned. He had managed to hold the box in his stomach for more than 30 hours.

All attempts to curb Tarrare's hunger failed, including opium and tobacco pills. In fact, Tarrare would break into medicine cabinets anyway, eating whatever he could find there. It was said that he became so hungry that he tried to drink the blood of fellow patients, and even started to chew on corpses in the hospital morgue.

When a young child disappeared from the building, suspicion fell on a ravenous Tarrare, and he was driven out of town. He died a few years later in Versailles, aged only 26, after suffering a bout of diarrhea, likely brought on by his extreme diet.

When a doctor performed an autopsy, he found that Tarrare's body was already rotting from the inside, and the smell was so bad that he could not continue the procedure. He did notice, however, how the patient's molar teeth were worn away by the unusual edibles he consumed, and how wide the mouth and gullet were—physiological features that may have helped the unfortunate Frenchman to eat so much.

Featured in:
- January 30, 1990 cartoon
- 2000 episode of the *Ripley's Believe It or Not!* TV show
- 2018 book *Odd Is Art*

45 Sketchy Artist

George Vlosich can create superbly detailed portraits and collages all on an ordinary Etch-A-Sketch! Each picture takes him up to 80 hours to draw using the toy's two dials—all in one unbroken line.

In 1989 the Vlosich family was about to set off on a trip from their home in Cleveland, Ohio, to Washington, D.C., but before they left they stopped over at George's grandparents' house to say goodbye. There, his mom retrieved her 1960s Etch-A-Sketch so that 10-year-old George and his brother would have something to play with in the car during the almost six-hour drive. George Etched an amazing picture of the U.S. Capitol Building, which so impressed his parents that his dad stopped at a gas station to take a picture of it before George erased it.

Drawing on the Etch came naturally to George and became a new way for him to express his artistic talents. The more he Etched, the better he got at drawing, and the more he drew, the better he Etched. He entered monthly contests sponsored by the manufacturer of the toy and kept winning.

Ohio Art became suspicious and sent a representative to check that he was really the artist. After confirming that he was legit, they sent him a new Etch-A-Sketch every month so he could work on new creations. He has since gone on to Etch some of the world's greatest athletes and celebrities, including The Beatles, Tiger Woods, Elvis Presley, Will Smith, Abraham Lincoln, Muhammad Ali, and Barack Obama.

He begins by drawing an image in his sketchbook, making sure it will fit on the Etch's 5 × 7 in (12.5 × 17.5 cm) screen. He then draws the lines of the picture on

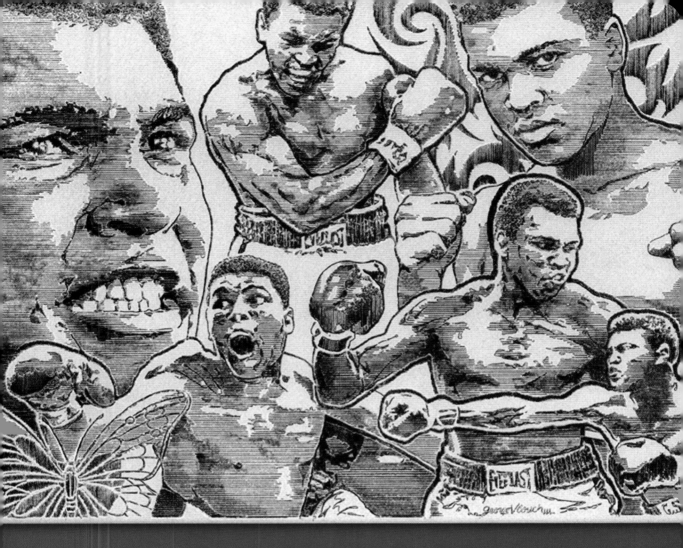

the Etch-A-Sketch and, because everything is done with a single line, if he makes a mistake, he has to start over.

After the lines have been Etched, he starts work on the shading, which is particularly time-consuming. Doing the shading from light to dark may require a single line to be traced as many as 30 times.

Once the picture is finished, he removes the aluminum powder and the stylus inside the toy to make sure it can never be erased. Every drawing is unique and cannot be duplicated.

George Vlosich's pictures are exhibited in art galleries throughout the world and they now sell for more than $10,000 each. His work has inspired others to pick up the art of Etching. Who would have thought that one man could achieve so much on a humble Etch-A-Sketch?

Zelma George
Zelma George
little bird told me
Charity begins

46 No Write Way

Zelma George, of Canton, Ohio, had an amazing ability—she not only could write both forward and backward, but also could write upside down and upside down backward! What's more, she could write a different sentence with each hand in any combination of upside down, backward, and so on simultaneously!

The talent that first brought Zelma George to the attention of Ripley's Believe It or Not! enabled her to outperform even the great Leonardo da Vinci. He was able to write both upside down and backward (or mirror writing as it is sometimes known), but there was no record of him being able to write different sentences with different hands at the same time.

He chose to write backward on a regular basis, starting from the right side of the page, partly to make it harder for other people to read his journals and copy his ideas, but also to avoid smudging his writing, because he was left-handed.

In particular, he sought to hide his scientific ideas from the powerful Catholic Church, whose teachings often conflicted with his observations. He only wrote in the normal direction from left to right when he wanted other people to read something.

Another notable person with a peculiar writing skill was U.S. President James Garfield who, in addition to being ambidextrous, could write a sentence simultaneously in Latin with one hand and in Greek with the other. He had previously taught both classical languages at Hiram College in Ohio before starting his political career.

PRESIDENT JAMES A. GARFIELD
COULD SIMULTANEOUSLY WRITE
LATIN WITH ONE HAND AND GREEK WITH THE OTHER

47

Fatal Coincidence

Featured in:
• March 25, 1990 cartoon

On July 30, 1974, 17-year-old Neville Ebbin was riding his moped in Sandys, Bermuda, when he was hit by a taxi and killed. Almost exactly one year later, on July 18, 1975, his younger brother Erskine, then 17 himself, was killed riding the same moped on a different stretch of the same road, by the same taxi, driven by the same man—and carrying the same taxi passenger.

SCREEEEEE

IN BERMUDA BROTHERS, ERSKINE L. EBBIN and NEVILLE EBBIN BOTH *DIED* ONE YEAR APART AFTER BEING STRUCK BY THE SAME TAXI DRIVEN BY THE SAME DRIVER AND CARRYING THE SAME *PASSENGER!*

48 Severed Skulls

Featured in:
• 2018 book *A Century of Strange!*

At the University of Lisbon in Portugal, you can see the severed head of a genuine serial killer.

Diogo Alves was hanged after murdering at least 70 people between 1836 and 1839. His modus operandi was to hide on a viaduct that ran into Lisbon from the countryside, seize unsuspecting farmers carrying their wares to market, and hurl them from the 200-ft-high (61-m) structure. After he changed his methods, breaking into a doctor's home and murdering the occupants, he was finally caught.

He was executed in 1841, and his head was severed and preserved in a jar for scientists to study. The pseudoscience of phrenology was popular at the time—it was thought by studying the head shapes of criminals, it would be possible to identify criminal personality traits. It's not known if Alves's skull was ever actually pored over by criminologists, but today he peacefully watches over the university's anatomical theatre.

Less than 100 years after Alves's execution, a serial killer known as "the Vampire of Düsseldorf" was spreading terror in Germany. In 1931 Peter Kürten was found guilty of nine counts of murder, plus seven counts of attempted murder—although some estimate the number of victims to be more than 30. He earned his nickname from his attempts to drink his victims' blood.

He was executed by guillotine, after which his head was dissected and mummified for study. It is now hanging at the Wisconsin Dells Odditorium, where guests can literally see into the head of a killer.

Featured in:
- **The Wisconsin Dells, Wisconsin, Odditorium**
- **2010 book *Enter If You Dare!***

Peter Kürten—the Vampire of Düsseldorf.

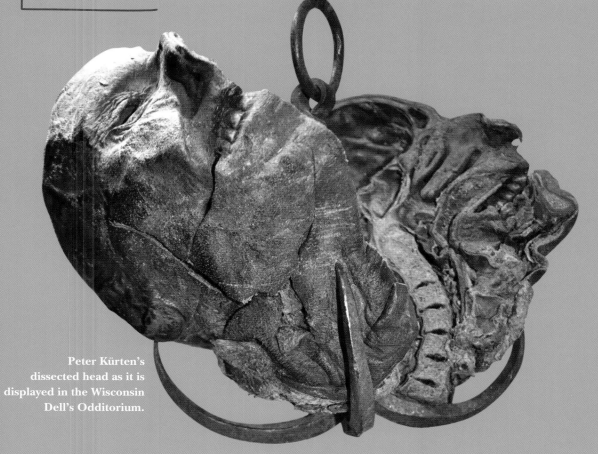

Peter Kürten's dissected head as it is displayed in the Wisconsin Dell's Odditorium.

NEW DIME MUSEUM

A SELECT FAMILY RESORT FOR LADIES AND CHILDREN.

Horticultural Hall Building, Tremont St., cor. Bromfield.

Open from 10 a. m. to 10 p. m. Daily.

FIRST APPEARANCE OF THE

MATCHLESS! INCOMPARABLE!

SEVEN

Sutherland Sisters

7 WONDERS OF THE WORLD!
7 LONG HAIRED SISTERS!
7 SONGSTERS!
7 ECCENTRIC LADIES!
7 ACCOMPLISHED MUSICIANS! 7
7 Refined and Educated Ladies!
7 SISTERS, ALL OF ONE FAMILY!
7 MODELS OF BEAUTY AND WOMANLY GRACE!
7 LADIES WITH 49 FEET OF HAIR!
7 FEET OF HAIR EACH!
7 Ladies with HAIR 4 INCHES THICK!

The Sutherland Sisters Entertain Visitors with Music Afternoon and Evening.

MLLE. ETTA.

THE WORLD AND ONLY

PHRENO - MNEMOTECHNIST!

FIRST-CLASS

STERLING ATTRACTIONS!

EVERYTHING NEW!   EVERYTHING ORIGINAL!

The Most Costly Curiosities!

RARE, BEAUTIFUL AND THE MOST

ECCENTRIC FREAKS!

ASTOUNDING ODDITIES!

Amazing OBJECTS of INTEREST!

Patronized by the Elite!
Endorsed by the Press!
Crowded by the Masses!

AMUSING OLD AND YOUNG!

ADMISSION 10 CTS.   SEATS FREE.

49

Seven Sutherland Sisters

Featured in:
- **June 7, 1981 cartoon**
- **2018 book *A Century of Strange!***

In the late 1800s, the Sutherland sisters were billed as "7 Wonders of the World! 7 Accomplished musicians! 7 Ladies with 49 feet of hair! 7 feet of hair each!"

The longhaired ladies, who came from humble beginnings on a turkey farm in upstate New York, had begun their life in show business as musicians. But Sarah, Victoria, Isabella, Grace, Naomi, Dora, and Mary happened to share 37 ft (11.3 m) of hair between them (sideshows would often exaggerate their performers' qualities), and while they were indeed talented singers and musicians, people didn't flock to see their skill so much as to see them let loose their luscious locks.

This was quite a spectacle, as while long hair was fashionable in the Victorian era, any respectable woman would always keep her hair up in polite society. The family began to market their hair more than their talents, and capitalized on the patent medicine trend by selling what they called "hair fertilizer" at their shows. They claimed that it was a secret lotion that their mother had used to make their tumbling tresses grow so long, but it was actually just a mixture of alcohol, oil, and water that they had recently invented.

Despite this, the concoction made them rich: along with other ointments and soaps, they netted $90,000 in sales the first year. When Naomi died in 1893, the family simply hired a replacement to keep the show on the road. The Sutherland Sisters fell out of favor when short bobbed hair became the fashion, but they still managed to make more than $2 million over their career. The girls used the money to build a mansion on the family farm, where they lived much of the rest of their lives together, as only two of the sisters ever married.

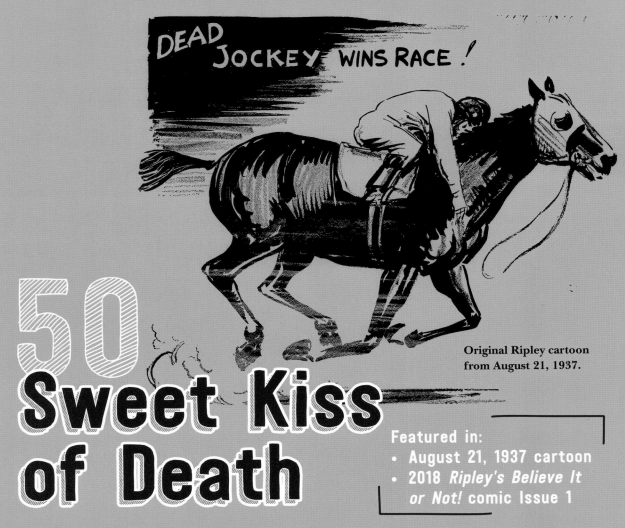

DEAD JOCKEY WINS RACE !

Original Ripley cartoon from August 21, 1937.

50
Sweet Kiss of Death

Featured in:
- August 21, 1937 cartoon
- 2018 *Ripley's Believe It or Not!* comic Issue 1

On June 4, 1923, Frank Hayes rode a horse called Sweet Kiss in a steeplechase at Belmont Park in New York. He won the race—a fact made amazing not by the 20-to-1 chances against him, but by the fact that he was dead!

Hayes was a part-time jockey who spent most of the time in the stables, and he had never won a race. Sweet Kiss was in the lead as she leapt the final fence, but Hayes was seen to sway and slump over in the saddle. He managed to remain in the stirrups, and Sweet Kiss didn't seem to notice, going on to win the race by a head.

When the horse's owner went to congratulate Hayes on his maiden win, the jockey dropped from the saddle, and to her horror she saw that he was dead. Hayes had suffered a heart attack in the middle of the race and had died before he even crossed the finish line.

Newspapers speculated that Hayes's death was caused by a combination of over-excitement at being in the lead, and a drastic weight loss program that saw him lose 12 lb (5.4 kg) in a short time in order to make the race.

CHAPTER 3
Animals

Koko the Gorilla

51

Artist Richard Stone with Koko as he works on his portrait of her.

K oko, a female western lowland gorilla, mastered sign language. She was able to make more than 1,000 signs and understand as many as 2,000 words of spoken English.

Koko was born at San Francisco Zoo in 1971, but after developing a serious illness she was sent to live with Francine Patterson, an animal psychologist. Patterson taught Koko a version of American Sign Language, which the gorilla used to convey her thoughts and feelings. Over time, Koko even invented signs to communicate new thoughts.

Patterson said that nobody taught Koko the word for "ring," but to refer to it, Koko combined the words "finger" and "bracelet" into "finger-bracelet."

Similarly, ice cream was "my cold cup" and her favorite nectarine yogurt became "orange flower sauce."

In regular IQ tests between 1972 and 1977, Koko scored between 70 and 90, which is comparable to a human infant.

By then Koko had moved to the Gorilla Foundation's preserve in Woodside, California, where she longed for a baby. When asked what present she wanted most, she would hold her elbows and rock from side to side, the sign for cradling an infant. If visitors showed her photos of their children, she would take the pictures and tenderly kiss their faces. In 1983, she used her signing skills to ask for a cat for Christmas. Presented with a stuffed toy, she

"KOKO," A LOWLAND GORILLA LIVING in San Francisco, Calif., CAN USE 1,000 DIFFERENT SIGNALS of AMERICAN SIGN LANGUAGE AND HAS WRITTEN SONG LYRICS THAT WERE RELEASED ON A CD.

appeared dissatisfied, did not play with it, and signed "sad."

On her birthday in July 1984, she was allowed to choose a real kitten, which she named "All Ball." She cared for the kitten as if it were her own baby. When All Ball was run over by a car after escaping from Koko's cage and Patterson signed to Koko that the kitten had been killed, the gorilla signed back "Bad, sad, bad" and "Frown, cry, frown, sad." Patterson also said she heard Koko make a sound like a human weeping.

Koko became a celebrity, appearing twice on the cover of *National Geographic* magazine. For the first cover photo in 1978, she held a camera and took her own picture in a mirror—one of the first-ever animal selfies. She also inspired a best-selling children's book and interacted with the likes of Robin Williams (whose glasses she played with), William Shatner, and Leonardo DiCaprio. Once, while listening to Patterson and another zoologist debating whether to label Koko a "juvenile" or an "adolescent," she interrupted in sign language: "No, me gorilla!"

Koko died in her sleep on the morning of June 19, 2018, at age 46, having changed the way that we perceive communication and emotion in great apes.

A young Koko signs "listen" to animal psychologist Francine Patterson.

Featured in:
- May 17, 1935 radio broadcast
- 2017 book *Shatter Your Senses!*
- 2018 anniversary book *Ripley's Believe It or Not! 100 Years*

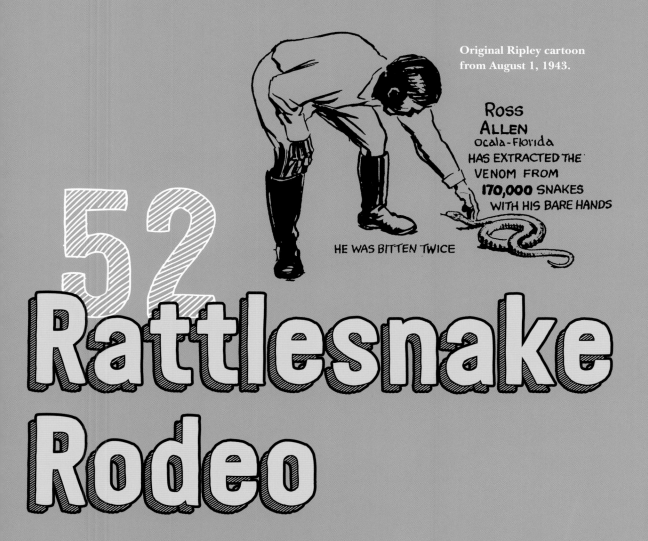

Original Ripley cartoon from August 1, 1943.

ROSS ALLEN Ocala-Florida HAS EXTRACTED THE VENOM FROM 170,000 SNAKES WITH HIS BARE HANDS

HE WAS BITTEN TWICE

52 Rattlesnake Rodeo

On May 17, 1935, at Silver Springs State Park in Silver Springs, Florida, Robert Ripley milked a rattlesnake on-air. A mishap occurred when Ripley climbed into a pit with 500 rattlesnakes with proprietor Ross Allen and the lights went out, prompting the professional snake handler to scream, "Let's get the hell outta here!" during the live broadcast.

Rattlesnake roundups and rodeos originated in the first half of the 20th century, partly to provide excitement and entertainment but also as a means of reducing the numbers of a species that were considered to be a pest as well as a danger. These days, roundups take place in at least 10 states and feature trade and food stalls, plus serious information about rattlesnake biology, identification, and safety.

The largest anywhere in the world is in Sweetwater, Texas, where every year more than 25,000 people come to watch and participate in the capture and beheading of thousands of diamondback rattlesnakes. In a good year, the roundup can capture 1% of the state's rattlesnake population.

Hunters used to flush the snakes out of their burrows by pouring in small amounts of harmful gasoline, which could damage other wildlife living down there, but today they prefer to ram stiff plastic tubes into the holes, put one ear to the end, and listen for rattling. If they hear something, they insert another tube with a treble hook tied to the end to pull the snake out.

The captured snakes are first displayed in a giant viewing pit, where handlers with protective gloves and long sticks stir the reptiles to keep them from suffocating. After the kill, no part of the snake goes to waste; the skin is turned into leather, the meat is fried up

Spectators young and old alike take part in skinning the rattlesnakes.

to be eaten, and the venom is extracted for research purposes.

This has to be done with great care, because people have received potentially deadly bites from the severed heads of rattlesnakes. This is because snakes—like many other reptiles—retain their reflexes for several hours after death and can bite if someone tries to pick up the head.

Reacting to concerns from environmentalists, some roundups now impose restrictions on the size and number of snakes caught, while others release the captured snakes back into the wild after the rodeo.

Ross Allen, Ripley's partner in the pit, was a born showman who entertained audiences at Silver Springs for 46 years. He conducted extensive research there to develop snake anti-venoms, which he himself needed on a dozen occasions after being bitten while milking rattlesnakes. The bites left the thumb on his left hand visibly deformed, and he often used to hide it in photos. He also used to wrestle alligators and anacondas... for fun.

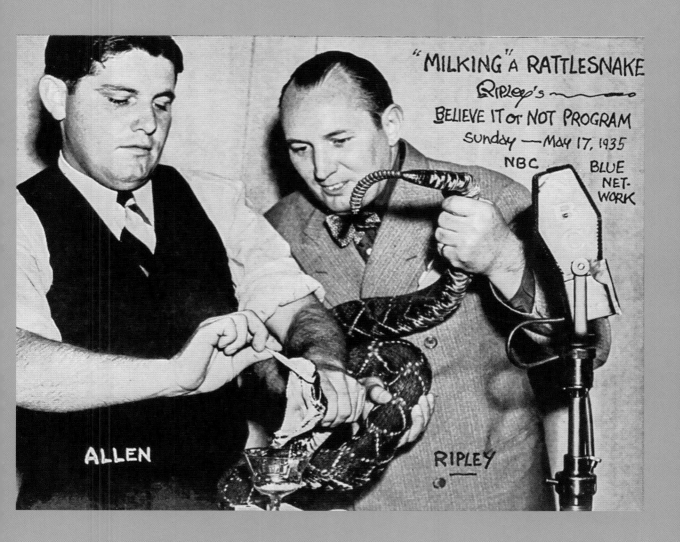

53

Whoa! Worm

In September 2009, American naturalist Stephen Hopkins found a gigantic worm—5 ft (1.5 m) long and with a girth the size of a man's arm—partly hidden under a rotten log in the foothills of the Sumaco Volcano in Ecuador.

The area is a remote tropical rain forest, where the untouched jungle is home to an array of bizarre creatures, especially weird worms. It is one of the wettest places in the world, and Hopkins and his local guide had been wading through mud for six hours when they caught sight of the monster. It was so big that Hopkins had no idea what it was, and nor did any of the experts he later asked for advice in identifying the giant.

It was the unusual thickness of the worm's body that stumped the scientists; there are several species of very long land worms, but none with the heft of Hopkins's Ecuadorian monster, which he estimated to have weighed about 2 lb (0.9 kg). The mystery earthworm has been categorized as part of the oligochaetes subclass of invertebrates, which includes earthworms, but is otherwise unidentified and could well be a previously undiscovered species.

54

Armed Armadillos

In April 2015, Larry McElroy of Lee County, Georgia, accidentally shot his mother-in-law after the bullet ricocheted off an armadillo.

The 9 mm ammo killed the armadillo, hit a fence, then flew through the back door of Carol Johnson's mobile home and passed through a reclining chair she was lying in, hitting her in the back. Luckily, she was not seriously injured.

Astonishingly enough, something similar happened just two years later. An unnamed man from Cass County, Texas, was hospitalized in August 2017 after a bullet he had fired at an armadillo on his property bounced off the animal and hit him in the head.

He was airlifted to the hospital, where his jaw had to be wired shut. The local sheriff said that the armadillo, which is considered a pest in southern states, was not located after the incident.

Tough Tortoise

55

One of the most curious natural exhibits in the Ripley's Believe It or Not! collection is a large tortoise with a huge hippopotamus tusk through its shell. What's more, it is believed that the sulcata spurred tortoise lived with the 2-ft-long (60-cm) tusk impaled in its shell for more than 15 years.

The tortoise was found dead in Zimbabwe in 2008. It was nearly 50 years old and was later preserved, as found, by a taxidermist. It is assumed that the hippo tried to bite the tortoise, but broke its tooth in the process. The third largest species of tortoise in the world, the sulcata spurred can reach 33 in (82.5 cm) long and weigh 231 lb (105 kg)—heavier than the average man.

As with all tortoises, its shell is very tough and is built to absorb attacks from predators that its body would otherwise have to deal with. Tortoises can

even survive attacks from crocodiles. Believe it or not, they are more at risk from large birds or smaller animals. Eagles have found that if they can lift a tortoise high into the air and then drop it, the shell will shatter on impact. And some small animals are able to eat their way into the tortoise's opening at the rear of the shell and chew its legs and tail.

The tortoise with its unusual appendage was seen by local natives for many years after the attack and continued to grow despite the presence of the tusk. The hippo may not have fared so well. The front incisors (or tusks) are its key weapons for inflicting wounds on rivals, and without one it could have been left vulnerable in combat.

Featured in:
- **Odditoriums around the world**

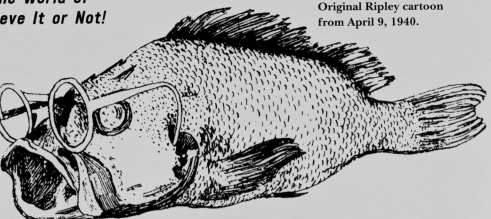

Original Ripley cartoon from April 9, 1940.

ROCK COD WEARING SPECTACLES
CAUGHT BY FRANK KENNEDY
LUMMI ISLAND
Washington

56

Fish Eyes

"A nearsighted rock cod was caught sporting spectacles in the waters off Bellingham, Washington. As if that were not enough, the glasses were identified by salesman Ira D. Erling as his own. It seems his glasses went overboard while he was out trolling for salmon in the same area where the fish was caught."—*Dear Mr. Ripley*

During the Great Depression, the Ripley's Believe It or Not! daily cartoons were read by more than 80 million people in 17 languages, in more than 300 newspapers. Robert Ripley encouraged readers to send in their own stories about the weird and the wonderful and received up to 3,500 letters every day, earning him the distinction, so it was claimed, of receiving more mail than any other person in history. As with this 1940 letter, most correspondents sent an accompanying photograph as proof that the submission was not simply a wild fabrication.

Nevertheless, this story may come into the "or not" category of "Believe It or Not!". It is a wonderful tale, but there is a possibility that the picture was staged by a reader eager to appear in a Ripley's cartoon and that the glasses were added after the fish was caught. Otherwise, surely they would have fallen off the cod's head as it was being hauled in. And even if it did somehow manage to slip into the glasses in the first place and keep them in perfect position, why did it continue wearing them? Unless, of course, they really did improve its eyesight or it thought that they made its eyes look bigger and more menacing to ward off potential predators. It may also have thought that no self-respecting seal or polar bear would attack a fish wearing glasses!

Then again, in the 2017 book *Shatter Your Senses!*, Ripley's did feature a true story about a hermit crab in the Maldives that lived in a discarded plastic cup. And in 2005, Florida angler Eric Bartos caught a fish that was wearing his wedding ring! Going through a divorce, he had put the ring over the bill of the same sailfish 25 months previously. So maybe the fish wearing spectacles wasn't so absurd after all.

57
Murderous Mary

Featured in:
- August 29, 1938 cartoon
- 2011 book *Strikingly True*

Original Ripley
cartoon from
August 29, 1938.

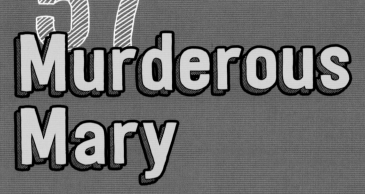

Mary was a 10,000-lb (4,500 kg) Asian elephant who was the star attraction for Sparks World Famous Shows in the early 20th century. When on tour, the showmen would whip up interest in local newspapers by spreading rumors that "Murderous Mary" was a dangerous creature that had actually killed several people already.

On September 12, 1916, in Kingsport, Tennessee, Mary finally lived up to her name. Stories of exactly how it transpired vary, but basically what happened was this: Performing in front of a packed crowd, Mary grabbed her trainer with her trunk, pinned him to the floor, and stomped on his head, killing him instantly. It was later revealed that the "trainer" was a drifter with no experience with animals, who had been hired only days previously. He angered Mary by poking the elephant repeatedly in the head with a spear-like tool while she was eating a watermelon rind. Mary also was said to have suffered from painful dental problems, which could help explain her aggressive response.

The horrified crowd panicked—one person shot Mary five times, but the bullets did not pierce her thick hide. People began to chant, "Kill the elephant," and so it was decided to hang her for her "crime." The next day, 2,500 people gathered to watch the gruesome execution. Mary was led to a crane in the nearby town of Erwin, where a chain was wrapped around her neck and they began to lift her up, forgetting that her leg had been shackled to the ground. The chain snapped and Mary fell, breaking her hip. A stronger chain was attached and her leg released from the ground. This time it worked, and Mary was soon dead.

In recent years, the town of Erwin, Tennessee, has held multiple events in memory of Mary for the purpose of raising money for a local elephant sanctuary.

58 Locked Horns

Featured in:
• 2018 book *A Century of Strange!*

In November 2016, schoolteacher Brad Webster came across a bizarre sight on a frozen lake near the remote village of Unalakleet, Alaska. Two bull moose were lying frozen on the surface, clearly having died mid-fight—their huge bodies mostly submerged and their antlers sticking out of the ice, still locked together.

A few days later, Webster showed the morbid scene to a friend of his, who had never seen anything like it, despite hunting in the area for 50 years. Occasionally moose skulls with entangled antlers are found, but experts have never seen them encased in ice. The battle likely took place at the end of the rutting season as the two males fought over a female. It's thought they may have fallen into the water while locked together and drowned. The men removed the heads, and then had the skulls cleaned and mounted in their original locked position.

59 Fancy Feathers

Featured in:
- June 5, 1928 cartoon
- Odditoriums as taxidermied examples

The Yokohama, or phoenix, is actually a German breed of chicken first bred in the late 19th century. They were descended from birds first shipped out from Yokohama, Japan, and known as Onagadori, an ornamental breed with exceptionally long tails.

The birds have been cultivated in Southwestern Japan since the mid-17th century, where they live in huts high off the floor so that their tails are not damaged by dragging on the ground. They are partly descended from wild Indonesian jungle fowl, whose feathers do not molt. The Onagadori shares the same gene, which is why their tails grow so long.

In June 1928, Robert Ripley's *Believe It or Not!* cartoon claimed that "A Yokohama rooster had a tail 21 feet long." In 1972 a rooster belonging to Masasha Kubota of Kochi in Japan had its tail feathers measured at 34 ft 9.5 in (10.6 m)—longer than a bus.

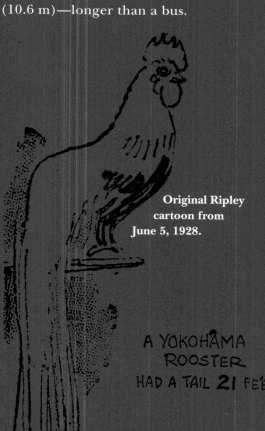

Original Ripley cartoon from June 5, 1928.

A YOKOHAMA ROOSTER HAD A TAIL **21** FEET LONG

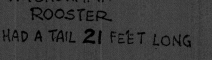

60 Bird Brain

Alex, an African gray parrot, could identify 50 different objects, seven colors, five shapes, and quantities up to six.

Alex came under the wing of animal psychologist Irene Pepperberg, who bought him at a pet store in 1977 when he was one year old and she was a researcher at Purdue University, Indiana. He would eventually develop a vocabulary of over 100 words, but it was his ability to understand language—rather than just repeat words—and do math that made him extraordinary. Pepperberg said he had an intellect equivalent to a five-year-old child and the emotional level of a two-year-old.

He took part in nearly 30 years of experiments at three American universities to test his intelligence levels. As well as being able to distinguish colors and shapes, Alex understood the concepts of "bigger," "smaller," "same," and "different." When shown an object and asked about its shape, color, or material, he could label it correctly. For example, when he was shown keys in different sizes, shapes, and colors, he was still able to identify each one as a key. He could also correctly identify the number of objects on a tray, demonstrating an ability either to count or to estimate accurately. Looking into a mirror, he would ask, "What color?," referring to himself. This made him the only non-human to have ever asked a question.

He insisted that Pepperberg greet him first every morning (before any of the other parrots at the facility) and would refuse to work with her that day if she didn't. When he was tired of being tested, he would say, "Wanna go back." If he said, "Wanna banana" but was offered a nut instead, he stared in silence before asking for the banana again. Or he would throw the nut at the researcher and then repeat his request for the banana.

He even seemed able to detect if Pepperberg was upset about something, because he would instinctively say "I love you." Once, he chewed through an important set of papers, leaving her distraught. He looked into her eyes and said, "I'm sorry... I'm sorry," even though she had never taught him those words. Then she recalled apologizing after becoming irritated with him once before when he had spilled a cup of coffee. He had obviously remembered that "I'm sorry" was the term used for defusing anger.

Alex died suddenly in 2007. His last words to Pepperberg were: "You be good. See you tomorrow. I love you." Years after his death, he still receives mail from his thousands of fans around the world.

Featured in:
- **June 17, 1990 cartoon**
- ***Ripley's Believe It or Not!* TV show in 2000**
- **2005 book *Top 10: Weirdest of the Weird***
- **2008 book *Prepare to Be Shocked!***

ALEX, AN AFRICAN GREY PARROT OWNED BY IRENE PEPPERBERG OF EVANSTON, IL, KNOWS THE NAMES OF 80 DIFFERENT OBJECTS AND CAN SORT THEM BY COLOR, SHAPE AND TEXTURE!

61 Skiing Squirrels

Like everyone else, Ripley's Believe It or Not! loves a talented pet story, and they don't come much cuter or more unusual than Twiggy the waterskiing squirrel.

It all started in 1978 when Chuck and Lou Ann Best, who ran a roller-skating rink in Sanford, Florida, were given an orphaned baby gray squirrel that had been blown from its nest by Hurricane David.

They decided to raise her as a family pet and were amazed to see how well she interacted with humans, nestling in Lou Ann's shirt to keep warm and joining the Bests on their water-skiing trips, where she would happily sit on their shoulders while they sat in the water. They named her Twiggy because she chewed the leaves off all of Lou Ann's house plants, leaving nothing but twigs.

One day, Chuck bought his daughter Lalainia a remote-controlled boat for her birthday, but, as with all dads, he loved to play with it himself. When his friends teased him about it, he joked: "I have to learn to drive the boat so I can teach my squirrel to water-ski!"

That throwaway line gave the Bests an idea—they really would teach their squirrel to water-ski! With a combination of affection, patience, and plenty of nuts, they taught Twiggy to stand on specially made plastic foam miniature skis and be towed around a 6-in-deep (15-cm) inflatable pool at speeds of up at 6 mph (9.6 kmph) by a toy boat. Pretty soon she was appearing on national TV and in shows across the country.

In 1997 Chuck Best had a heart attack and drowned while saving the life of his stepfather. The original Twiggy had long since passed away. Lou Ann was unsure whether to continue with the act, but one afternoon, while she was sitting in her dining room, a squirrel appeared at her door. She let the squirrel into the house, dubbed her Twiggy II, and soon started with water-skiing training in the bathtub.

Chuck's tragic death encouraged Lou Ann to make water safety an important part of the act and she created a squirrel-sized lifejacket for Twiggy to wear in her shows. In time, Hollywood stardom beckoned, too, with Twiggy demonstrating her unique skills in *Dodgeball: A True Underdog Story* and *Anchorman: The Legend of Ron Burgundy*.

There have been eight Twiggys, because not even talented pets live forever, and in 2018, after four decades, Lou Ann decided it was time to take her on her farewell tour.

Apart from water-skiing, Twiggy has learned to hang-glide, jet ski, and ride in a helicopter.

RING RING RING! WOOF WOOF!

62 Lyre Liar

The Australian lyrebird can mimic the sounds of as many as 25 other bird species, as well as imitate animals such as koalas and dingoes and a whole range of human noises, including chainsaws, car engines, trains, car alarms, fire alarms, rifle shots, camera shutters, human voices, crying babies, and cell phone ring tones.

The superb lyrebird's ability to mimic almost any sound it hears is thought to stem from the makeup of its vocal organ, or syrinx. Whereas other songbirds have four pairs of syringeal muscles, the lyrebird only has three, making it more flexible. It sings with the greatest intensity at the peak of the breeding season, from June to August, and up to 80% of its song consists of mimicry. Its repertoire is truly amazing.

One notable instance of its incredible mimicry appeared in the 1982 book *Ripley's Believe It or Not! Book of Australia and New Zealand*. It told the story of a Scotsman living in Monaro, New South Wales, who practiced his bagpipes each night. When he passed, his neighbors were terrified to hear the music continue! It turned out the "ghost" was actually a lyrebird, who had learned to imitate the man's notes exactly.

Nobody really knows why the lyrebird needs such a vast repertoire. Unlike the drongo, which makes fake alarm calls to induce animals and other birds to flee and give up their hard-earned food, there is no evidence to suggest that the lyrebird actively tries to fool other species. Some experts believe it uses its song simply to intimidate rivals in the forest.

It has even been claimed that a pet lyrebird whose owner used to play the flute in the 1920s retained the musical sounds after being released back into the wild in New South Wales—and that its descendants were still singing tunes from that period more than 40 years later.

Featured in:
- **Various cartoons over the past century**
- **1982 book *Ripley's Believe It or Not! Book of Australia and New Zealand***
- **1983 episode of the *Ripley's Believe It or Not!* TV show**

The lyrebird gets its name from its elaborate tail feathers which, when on full display, look like a lyre. It is a happy coincidence that "lyre" and "liar" sound alike.

63

Sea Turtles

A 4-ft-long (1.2-m) loggerhead sea turtle created entirely from magazine pages!

Candelaria Villanueva, thrown into the sea when an inter-island Philippine passenger ship sank 600 mi (966 km) south of Manila, was kept afloat for two days by a giant sea turtle! Villanueva was riding the turtle's back when she was sighted by a rescue ship.

After her boat sank in 1974, 52-year-old Villanueva said she had been floating in the water for more than 12 hours when a sea turtle "with a head as big as that of a dog" appeared beneath her. When she was eventually spotted 36 hours later, her rescuers thought she was clinging to an oil drum. As soon as they threw her a life ring, the "drum" sank.

One said: "We did not realize it was a giant turtle until we started hauling up the woman, for the turtle was beneath her, apparently propping her up. It even circled the area twice before disappearing into the depths of the sea, as if to reassure itself that its former rider was in good hands."

Sea turtles have long been a source of wonderment to Ripley's Believe It or Not! The oldest known sea turtle fossil dates back about 150 million years, making them among the oldest creatures on the planet, and an individual specimen has been known to live for 188 years. Yet the infant mortality rate is alarmingly high.

Only one out of every 100 eggs laid by a female lives for a year, and only one out of every 1,000 eggs will reach adulthood. On average, a female green sea turtle will lay 1,800 eggs during her lifetime, but only 374 will hatch and only a couple of those will live long enough to breed.

The loggerhead has the largest head of all sea turtle species. This skull is on display at the Orlando, Florida, Odditorium.

On hatching, a baby sea turtle swims 50 mi (80 km) out to sea, where for a year it rides on floating seaweed, eating crabs, shrimp, and jellyfish until it reaches maturity. Typically, a sea turtle increases its weight by 6,000 times as it grows from hatchling to adult. It can hold its breath underwater for five hours, and if threatened can swim at speeds of up to 22 mph (35 kmph).

When it's time to lay eggs, the female instinctively returns to the same nesting grounds where she was born, even if it means swimming 3,000 mi (4,800 km)—equal to crossing the Atlantic Ocean—to get there. Leatherback sea turtles can travel more than 10,000 mi (16,000 km) every year.

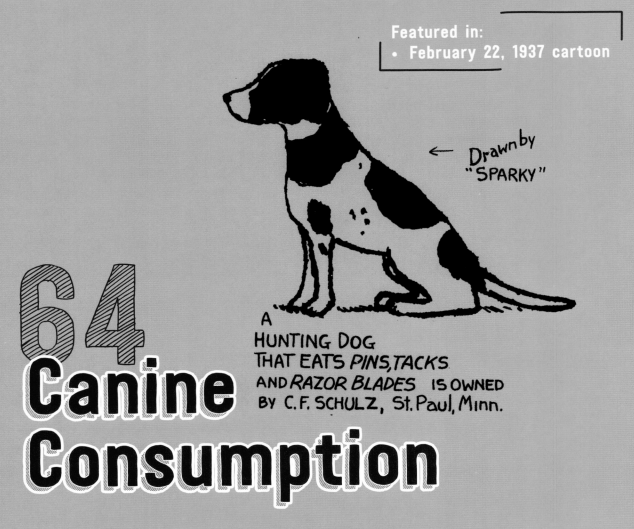

← Drawn by "SPARKY"

A HUNTING DOG THAT EATS *PINS, TACKS* AND *RAZOR BLADES* IS OWNED BY C.F. SCHULZ, St. Paul, Minn.

64
Canine Consumption

On February 22, 1937, the Ripley's cartoon featured a sketch of Spike, "A hunting dog that eats pins, tacks, and razor blades is owned by C. F. Schulz, St. Paul, Minn." For once, the drawing was not one of Ripley's—it was submitted by a 15-year-old Charles Schulz.

It was the budding cartoonist's first professional publication, and Spike would later become the inspiration for "Snoopy" in Schulz's legendary comic strip *Peanuts*. Ever since then, Ripley's has featured dogs' impressively indiscriminating appetites, and their remarkable ability to survive eating the inedible.

In 2014, a three-year-old Great Dane owned by a family in Oregon ate 43 socks! When the dog began repeatedly vomiting and retching, it was taken to DoveLewis Emergency Animal Hospital in Portland, where an X-ray showed the poor pup's belly completely stuffed. Luckily, the vet was able to remove all of the offending garments, and the dog made a full recovery.

The 43 socks removed from the stomach of a Great Dane in 2014!

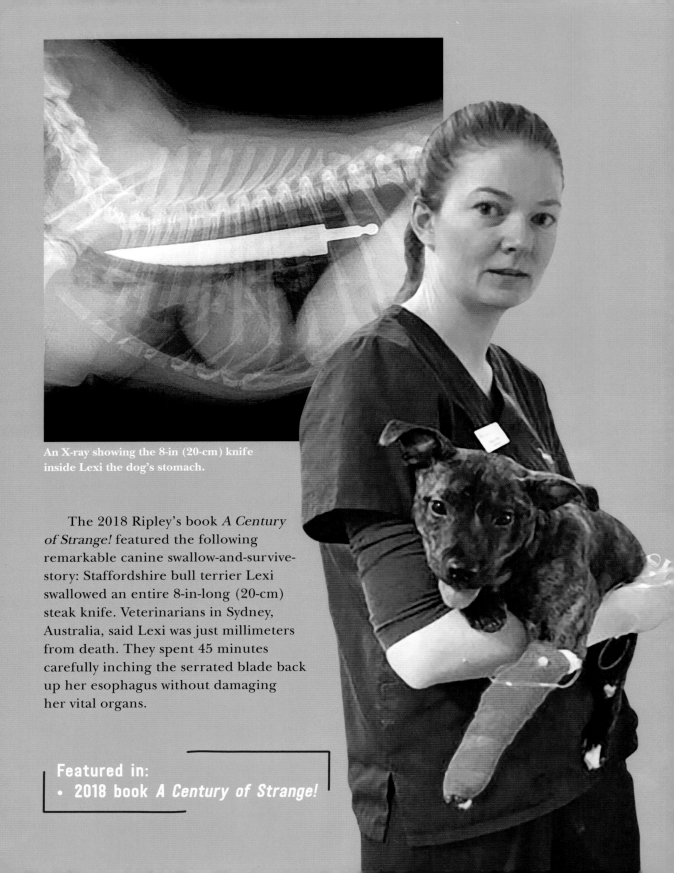

An X-ray showing the 8-in (20-cm) knife inside Lexi the dog's stomach.

The 2018 Ripley's book *A Century of Strange!* featured the following remarkable canine swallow-and-survive-story: Staffordshire bull terrier Lexi swallowed an entire 8-in-long (20-cm) steak knife. Veterinarians in Sydney, Australia, said Lexi was just millimeters from death. They spent 45 minutes carefully inching the serrated blade back up her esophagus without damaging her vital organs.

Featured in:
• 2018 book *A Century of Strange!*

CHAPTER 4

World

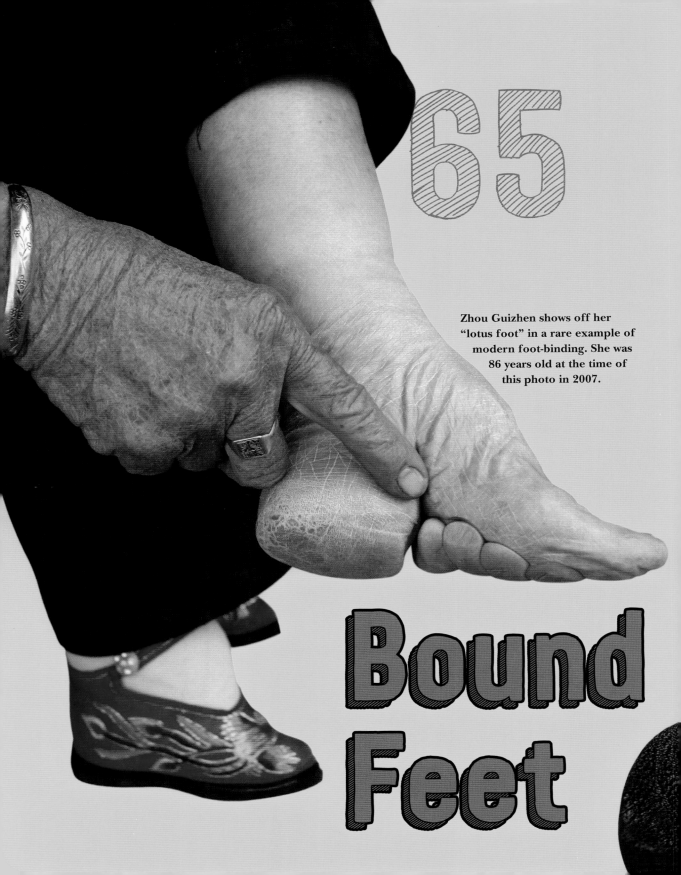

65

Zhou Guizhen shows off her "lotus foot" in a rare example of modern foot-binding. She was 86 years old at the time of this photo in 2007.

Bound Feet

For centuries, upper-class Chinese women would undergo the painful ritual of foot binding. Chosen girls would have their feet first bound when they were very young—between four and ten—before the arch of the foot had fully developed.

Their feet were washed, sometimes in animal blood, and the four smallest toes were broken and then curled over and down under the ball of the foot. The toes were secured by tight silk bindings that wrapped around the ankle. Bindings were regularly removed and then tightened in a process that lasted several years.

The bound-foot ideal was a highly exaggerated arch to the sole so that the toes and ball of the foot almost touched the heel. The result, known as "lily" or "lotus" feet, was deemed attractive and symbolic of wealth and breeding, and special silk slippers were worn.

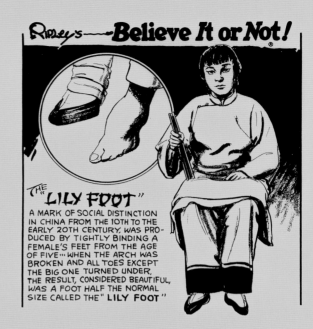

Ripley's—Believe It or Not!

THE "LILY FOOT"

A MARK OF SOCIAL DISTINCTION IN CHINA FROM THE 10TH TO THE EARLY 20TH CENTURY, WAS PRODUCED BY TIGHTLY BINDING A FEMALE'S FEET FROM THE AGE OF FIVE… WHEN THE ARCH WAS BROKEN AND ALL TOES EXCEPT THE BIG ONE TURNED UNDER, THE RESULT, CONSIDERED BEAUTIFUL, WAS A FOOT HALF THE NORMAL SIZE CALLED THE "LILY FOOT"

Featured in:
- **Odditoriums around the world**
- **Episode of *Ripley's Believe It or Not!* TV show in 2000**

It is not clear exactly how feet binding came about, but the practice is more than 1,000 years old. The practice was most popular during the Tang Dynasty, but girls were still having their feet bound into early 20th century. Initially encouraged by the upper classes, it would spread across the whole of Chinese society.

The deformity made walking almost impossible, so women with bound feet were usually carried from place to place in a chair or reclining on a bed. This demonstrated how Chinese women were expected to let men do everything for them, but it was also used as a way to keep women at home.

66 Bovine Beverage

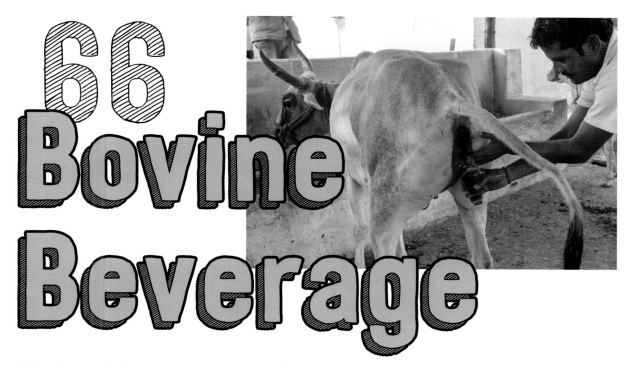

Hindu worshippers at Mr. Singhal's Agra Gaushala Foundation in Agra, India, believe that drinking fresh cow urine first thing in the morning can cure stomach problems, cancer, and diabetes. They also claim that cow pee is the only effective treatment for baldness.

Featured in:
• **2015 book *Eye-Popping Oddities!***

Hindus regard the cow as holy, and dozens of people gather every day to drink the animals' urine, although apparently for the medicine to work, the cow must not have given birth. Devotee Jairam Singhai has been drinking cow pee for more than 10 years and says it has brought his diabetes levels under control.

The power of cow urine is supported by Ayurvedic medicine, an ancient system of treatments originating more than 3,000 years ago in ancient Hindu texts. But it's not just the most highly religious that are interested in bovine pee products. Some alternative medical companies are collecting hundreds of thousands of gallons of bovine urine a day to make into cosmetics, including facial cream and soap. It's so valuable that farmers will stay up all night so that they can catch their cows when they need to "go."

Indians of the Jain religion also believe in the power of cow urine. At Jain's Cow Urine Therapy Health Clinic in Indore, 20 doctors provide therapies based on cow urine that claim to treat almost any ailment conceivable, from skin diseases to blood pressure, obesity, hemorrhoids, asthma, and heart problems.

In 2018 it was announced that a government pharmacy in Uttar Pradesh, India, was preparing to process and sell bottles of cow urine as a health drink.

Opposite page: A festival participant holds up an umbrella that is pierced through his tongue.

Featured in:
- 2013 book *Download the Weird*
- June 9, 2000 cartoon

67 Phuket Vegetarian Festival

At the annual Phuket Vegetarian Festival in Thailand, Taoist devotees self-mutilate by piercing dozens of sharp implements through their arms, legs, back, cheeks, and even their tongues as a way of purging evil spirits and bringing good luck to the community.

The mutilation is performed at more than 40 local Buddhist temples during what is also known as the Nine Emperor Gods Festival. The disciples undergo the agonizing ritual in a trancelike state, and then take part in street processions, displaying their injuries. They believe that the Chinese gods will protect them from the pain.

Tree branches, kebab skewers, kitchen knives, and needles are just some of the tools used for piercing. Among the more unusual are bicycles, palm fronds, guns, and umbrellas! Other wince-inducing feats include walking on hot coals, slashing the skin with swords, climbing ladders of sharp blades, and standing next to exploding firecrackers.

Participants abstain from meat and other luxuries during the ninth lunar month of the Chinese calendar, in the belief that abstinence will bring good luck and good health.

ADOLESCENTS

BEING INITIATED INTO MANHOOD BY PAPUA NEW GUINEA TRIBES OF THE SEPIK RIVER AREA, UNTIL THE 1930s UNDERWENT ELABORATE CEREMONIES DURING WHICH THEY WORE GROTESQUE MASKS AND WERE SCARRED *WITH CROCODILE TEETH*

68 Crocodile Skin

Young men of the Iatmul group, who live in villages along the Sepik River in Papua New Guinea, undergo a traditional "crocodile cutting" ceremony as a rite of passage to mark the end of their childhood. It typically involves males from the age of puberty, but sometimes they are much older.

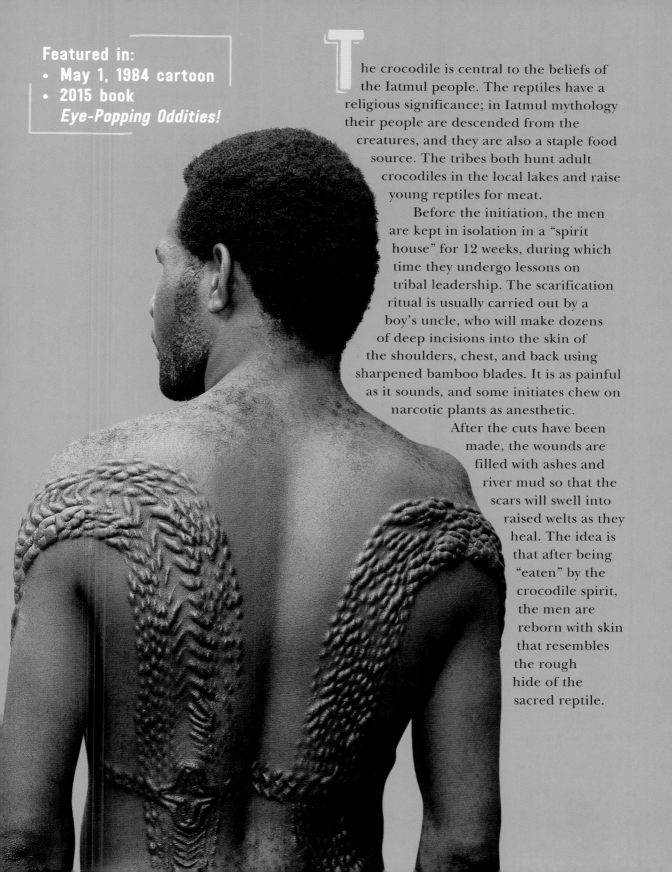

The crocodile is central to the beliefs of the Iatmul people. The reptiles have a religious significance; in Iatmul mythology their people are descended from the creatures, and they are also a staple food source. The tribes both hunt adult crocodiles in the local lakes and raise young reptiles for meat.

Before the initiation, the men are kept in isolation in a "spirit house" for 12 weeks, during which time they undergo lessons on tribal leadership. The scarification ritual is usually carried out by a boy's uncle, who will make dozens of deep incisions into the skin of the shoulders, chest, and back using sharpened bamboo blades. It is as painful as it sounds, and some initiates chew on narcotic plants as anesthetic.

After the cuts have been made, the wounds are filled with ashes and river mud so that the scars will swell into raised welts as they heal. The idea is that after being "eaten" by the crocodile spirit, the men are reborn with skin that resembles the rough hide of the sacred reptile.

69 Bulldogging

In the late 1970s and 1980s, thousands of deer lived in the forests of the Southern Alps mountain range of Fiordland, New Zealand. A non-native species, the deer had become something of a pest after being introduced in the 19th century. The hungry animals would eat so many young shoots that the forests were at risk.

In the 1930s, the government announced a cull, paying hunters to shoot the deer. In the 1970s, some deerstalkers started to hunt for live animals to domesticate, building the country's first deer farms. But taking the animals alive was easier said than done. Four-wheel drive vehicles were out of the question; the terrain was too rough, so moving the deer by air was the only option.

Helicopters were the chosen tool, being already popular with hunters who would shoot deer from the air, so for several years deer farmers joined up with pilots to fly low through the narrow fjords and scour the mountainsides in a search for new stock. When they found deer, the pilot would swoop down over the animals, and the stalkers would shoot giant nets over the fleeing animals before leaping out of the chopper and securing them with a large net. The helicopter would then return to

pick up the heavy cargo and transport it to its new home. Sometimes hunters just jumped onto the animals, wrestling them to the ground and tying their legs up, ready for lift-off. This daring technique became known as "bulldogging."

Bulldogging was as dangerous as it sounds, for both hunters and pilots. In six years between 1976 and 1982, there were more than 200 chopper crashes in Fiordland, and 17 lives were lost. But the risk was worth it, with a single live hind worth $3,000 to a venison farmer. It wasn't only the landscape and the deer they were fighting; venison was so profitable that bull-doggers began to clash over territory in what was called the "venison wars," sometimes leading to violent confrontation in the skies over the fjords. But those who persisted were highly successful, and today New Zealand has more than half the world's domesticated deer population, more than one million animals.

Featured in:
- 2001 episode of *Ripley's Believe It or Not!* TV show
- July 24, 2008 cartoon
- 2010 book *Enter If You Dare!*

CASU MARZU, A CHEESE MADE WITH LIVING MAGGOTS, IS STILL MADE IN NORTHERN ITALY ALTHOUGH IT IS ILLEGAL TO SELL IT!

70 No Cheese, Please

Casu Marzu cheese is a gourmet tradition on the island of Sardinia, Italy. While many cheeses encourage the growth of bacteria, Casu Marzu is not ready to eat until it is fully infested with the maggot larvae of the cheese fly.

As the larvae process the cheese, they give it the required moist texture, and then it is eaten, maggots and all. It is only when the bugs die that the cheese becomes unfit for human consumption!

The tiny 0.3 in (8 mm) long maggots that infest the cheese can jump 6 in (150 mm) when disturbed—the equivalent of an Olympic high jump champion leaping 126 ft (38 m).

What a Mouthful

71

Featured in:
- 2008 book *Prepare to Be Shocked!*
- April 30, 1933 cartoon

LANFAIRPWLLGW

Robert Ripley traveled the world in search of the bizarre, and in 1931 his adventures took him to a village on the small island of Anglesey off the northwest coast of Wales. The village has a 58-letter name, making it the longest place name in Europe and the second-longest in the world, behind an 85-letter location on New Zealand's North Island.

Llanfairpwllgwyngyllgogerychwyrndrobwllllantysiliogogogoch means "St. Mary's Church in the hollow of the white hazel near the rapid whirlpool and the church of St. Tysilio with a red cave." A settlement has existed on the site since at least 2000 BC, but it was known simply as "Llanfair Pwllgwyngyll" until the 1860s when a shoemaker from a nearby village suggested an extended version so that the village could boast having the longest name of any railway station in Britain. Little did he know that he had created one of the most successful marketing ideas of all time.

The move brought in the desired tourists but also meant that the station sign had to be closely guarded to stop visitors stealing it as a souvenir!

The full name featured as a secret password in the 1968 Jane Fonda movie *Barbarella*, and in 2011 was included in the new Anglesey version of the board game Monopoly. The makers said their biggest problem was fitting the entire name into a single square. For the same reason, signposts directing visitors to the village use the shortened "Llanfairpwllgwyngyll."

Most people steer clear of trying to pronounce the notorious tongue-twister and simply refer to it as "Llanfair PG," but in 2015, when Welsh TV weatherman Liam Dutton successfully pronounced the full name during a forecast, the video accumulated more than five million views on YouTube within 24 hours.

Furthermore, by adding uchaf.org.uk to the end of the full name, the village website also has the longest valid domain name in the world!

Featured in:
- 1982 episode of *Ripley's Believe It or Not!* TV show
- April 29, 2007 cartoon
- Odditoriums as scale model replicas

72

Subterranean Soldiers

In 210 BC Qin Shi Huang, the first emperor of China and ruler of the Qin Dynasty, died. When he was laid to rest in his mausoleum, he was joined by thousands of life-sized soldiers made from terra-cotta clay, whose job it was to protect the emperor in the afterlife.

The inanimate army consists of around 8,000 soldiers, varying in height according to their rank, and some 500 clay horses pulling hundreds of genuine bronze war chariots. The figures themselves are finely detailed, sharing about 10 different faces and standing in a variety of poses.

Although the existence of a great "necropolis"—a city for the dead—in which the emperor was buried was known from ancient historical texts, the sources made no mention of the figurines. Fragments of terra-cotta figures had been found in the area of Mount Li for hundreds of years, but their significance was not realized, and the emperor's incredible tomb lay undiscovered until 1974, when farmers in Shaanxi province were digging a well close to Mount Li.

Of the four main pits found, the largest contains 6,000 terra-cotta soldiers, and is so big that the Seattle Space Needle could fit on its side within. The next pit includes archers, cavalry, and charioteers, and the third, smallest pit contains the commanding officers. The fourth pit is empty, as construction halted due to uprisings a year after Qin's death.

The soldiers would have been originally brightly painted in multicolored detail, but most of the pigment disappeared within minutes of being unearthed. In 1987 the terra-cotta army was declared a World Heritage Site, and more figures are still being discovered, with 114 more clay warriors unearthed in 2010.

CHINA'S FIRST EMPEROR, QIN SHI HUANGDI (260 - 210 BC) WAS BURIED WITH A LIFE-SIZED ARMY OF 8,000 TERRA COTTA WARRIOR STATUES — EACH WITH AN INDIVIDUAL LOOK!

Featured in:
- December 5, 1969 cartoon
- July 24, 2012 cartoon

73
Bejeweled Bugs

In Central America, the makech beetle has been worn as jewelry for centuries. In the Yucatan region of Mexico, the live bugs are sold decorated in sparkling multicolor stones, finished with a gold chain that doubles up as a leash to prevent the insects from wandering off.

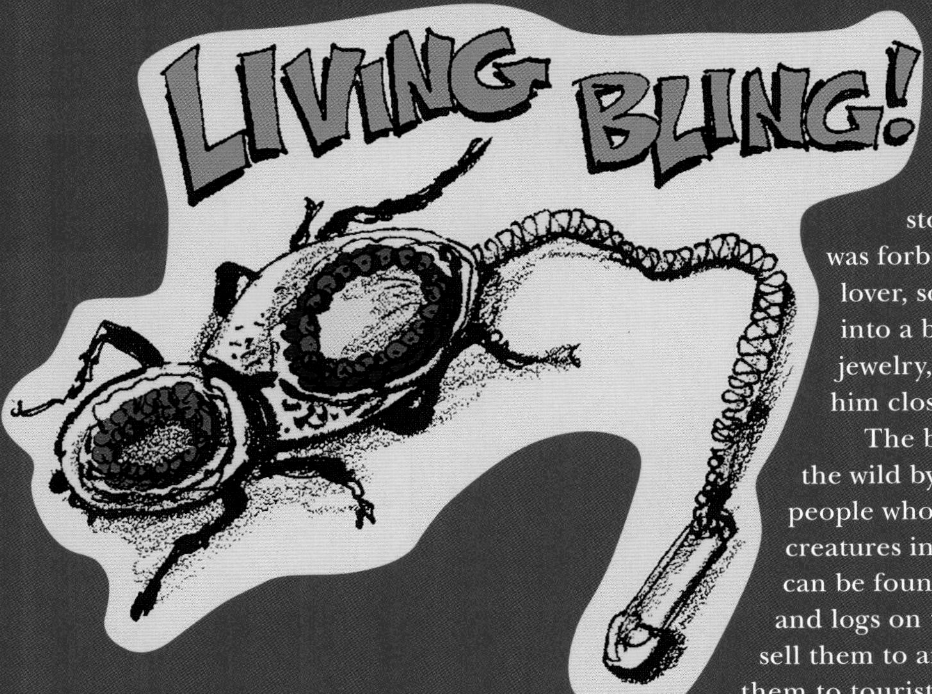

LIVING BLING!

Generally, they are worn as living brooches on a lapel or collar. Legend has it that the tradition has its origins in an ancient love story. A Mayan princess was forbidden from seeing her lover, so she had him turned into a beetle disguised as jewelry, so that she could keep him close to her heart.

The bugs are collected in the wild by "Los Maquecheros," people who specialize in finding the creatures in forests, where they can be found in rotting leaf litter and logs on the forest floor. They sell them to artists, who in turn sell them to tourists.

74
The Sourtoe
Cocktail

Bold customers of the Downtown Hotel in Dawson City, Yukon, Canada, can consume the Sourtoe cocktail—a drink featuring, believe it or not, a preserved human toe.

The rules say that while downing the drink the customer must touch the pickled toe with their lips. The 45-year-old tradition began in 1973 after the frostbitten toe of a former proprietor was found in a nearby cabin. Since then more than 60,000 people have tasted the unique cocktail, including an unfortunate man who accidently swallowed the toe in 1980.

Since then more than 10 additional toes have been donated to the bar to help carry on the tradition. In 2013, a U.S. man swallowed the sour toe on purpose in a bizarre display of bravado. Instead of just touching the toe to his lips, this customer swished it into his mouth, followed it with a beer, and then slapped $500 onto the bar—the hotel's fine for toe-swallowing.

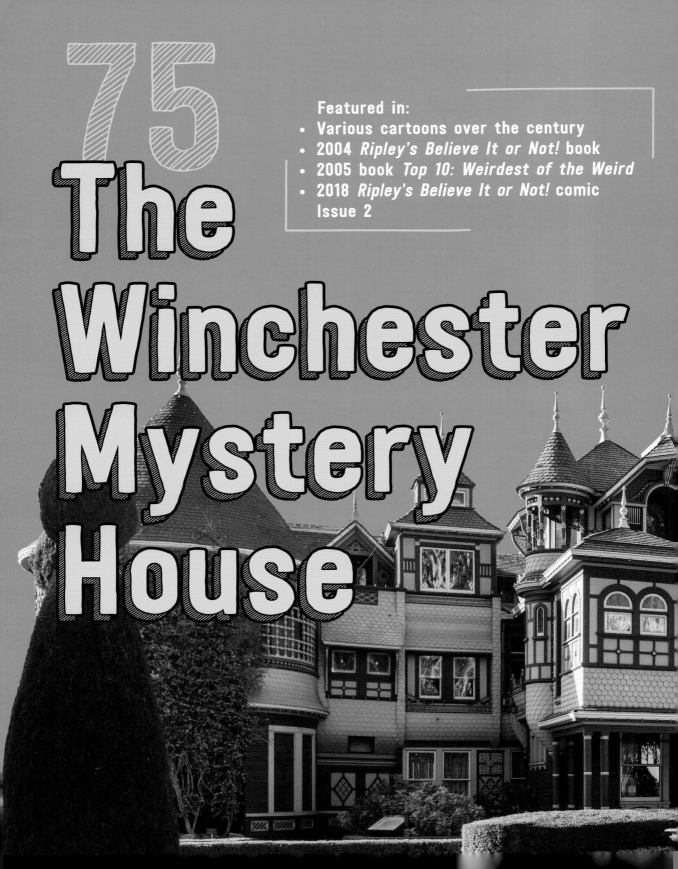

75

The Winchester Mystery House

Featured in:
- Various cartoons over the century
- 2004 *Ripley's Believe It or Not!* book
- 2005 book *Top 10: Weirdest of the Weird*
- 2018 *Ripley's Believe It or Not!* comic Issue 2

Sarah Winchester, wealthy widow of the rifle tycoon William Winchester, spent 38 years building what may be the most puzzling house ever. Baffling in both its bizarre design and unknown inspiration, the "Winchester mystery house" in San Jose, California, is a gigantic mansion with staircases that go nowhere, doors that open onto walls, dead-end corridors, and inaccessible balconies.

Why the house was built, and in such an unusual fashion, is still a mystery. What is known is that Sarah Winchester was devastated by the deaths of her daughter and husband, and felt compelled to move from Connecticut to the Santa Clara Valley in order to build a home. And she didn't finish building until she died. Legend has it that Sarah's spirit guides told her that she must build continuously in order to appease the spirits of people killed by Winchester rifles, which are said to still haunt the house.

The mansion began as an unfinished farmhouse and never had an architect's plan; it was built room-by-room according to the owner's whims. From 1884 to 1922, builders and carpenters were kept busy every day. Sarah inherited a vast fortune after her husband's death, meaning money for construction was never a problem. The building featured contemporary luxuries

such as elevators, electric lighting, and showers. It was filled with fine furniture, and many of the rooms are decorated with intricately carved hardwood paneling.

It's said that Winchester's superstitions influenced a haphazard "design" intended to confuse wandering spirits. Many of the windows have 13 sheets of glass, and the number 13 reoccurs throughout the building. There are 13-panel ceilings, and many of the 40 staircases had 13 steps. There are 13 bathrooms, although only one was used; the rest were dummies to befuddle the resident ghosts.

The unfinished nature of the maze-like building and its deliberately confusing

design made it hard to map its features accurately. A new attic room fitted with a Victorian organ and sewing paraphernalia was only discovered in 2016. It's thought that the space had been boarded up following the 1906 San Francisco earthquake. The earthquake reduced the house from seven stories to four after a tower collapsed, and it was never built higher again.

By the end of Sarah's life, the mysterious mansion boasted 160 rooms, including nine kitchens and at least 40 bedrooms. This allowed Sarah to sleep in a different room every night in order to throw vengeful spirits off course. The house has 2,000 doors, not all of which are functional, and thousands of windows, including some that open into internal rooms, and skylights that don't let in any light. Winchester spent a fortune on custom stained-glass panes with spider web designs made by the Tiffany diamond company, and then kept them in the dark.

When Sarah died in 1922, aged 82, all building work stopped immediately—it's said that nails were left half-hammered into walls—and today the house is still unfinished.

Sarah Winchester's will was written in 13 sections and she signed it 13 times!

Mrs. Sarah Winchester – Only known portrait in existence. 1217

A woman poses on the infamous "stairway to nowhere."

76 The Burning Ghats

Featured in:
- Ripley's Ramble 'Round the World newspaper feature in 1923
- Many cartoons over the past century
- The very first *Ripley's Believe It or Not!* book in 1929
- 2018 anniversary book *Ripley's Believe It or Not! 100 Years*

In 1923 Robert Ripley's four-month global adventure took him to the Indian holy city of Benares, also known as Varanasi, which he immediately hailed as the most wonderful city in the world. "I have traveled 20,000 miles," he wrote, "and have seen no place which so baffles description as this."

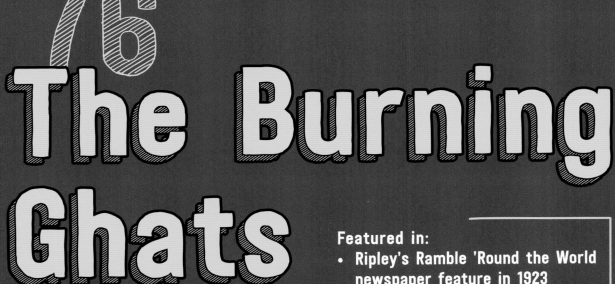

Ripley found India to be beguiling and baffling in equal measure, and nowhere more so than Benares, an ancient city that attracts thousands of pilgrims every year and is considered the most holy place on Earth for Hindus. He witnessed the ceremonial cremations that still take place along the banks of the sacred River Ganges, where devout Hindus come to wash away their sins by bathing in—and even drinking—the same water in which human ashes have just been scattered.

As many as 300 people are cremated there every day because it is believed that anybody whose ashes are scattered at the site will have their souls liberated and achieve nirvana. Wrapped in a colorful shroud, the corpse is carried through the streets on a bamboo stretcher and then immersed in the Ganges before being laid out to dry on the ghats, or steps, that lead down to the river. The bodies are burned on piles of wooden logs, and it is said that the flames of the funeral pyres at Manikarnika Ghat, the city's largest cremation site, have been burning for 3,000 years.

Elsewhere in the city, Ripley observed deeply religious sadhus demonstrating their faith by performing all manner of extreme disciplines, which earned their own spot in the 100 Best BIONS list. In home-movie footage, Ripley looks on in awe as a man pierces his own tongue with a bicycle spoke. "Nowhere on earth," wrote Ripley, "can you see such a weird cross-cut of human life."

77

Panama Perspective

Panama is the only country in the world where you can watch the sun rise over the Pacific Ocean and set over the Atlantic!

This is because Panama snakes around geographically in an S-shaped isthmus so that in Central Panama the Pacific Ocean (the Gulf of Panama) is located to the east, where the sun rises, and the Atlantic (the Caribbean Sea) is to the west, where the sun sets. Since the country is only 37 mi (60 km) wide at its narrowest, you can watch both spectacles without needing to travel far.

The country's unique shape also means that if you travel through the Panama Canal from the Pacific to the Atlantic you actually travel west rather than east—and similarly if you go from the Atlantic to the Pacific you travel east instead of west!

Ripley probably picked up these nuggets of information when he visited Panama in 1925 as part of his "Ramble 'Round South America," an expedition which promised that his readers would "learn things about South America that are not found in books."

More than 25,000 workers died during the construction of the Panama Canal, mainly from tropical disease. As many as 15,000 ships use the canal every year—an average of 40 a day—and each pays a toll based on its weight. In 2008, a Disney cruise ship paid a toll of $330,000. The smallest toll ever collected was 36 cents, paid by American adventurer Richard Halliburton, who swam the canal in 1928.

CHAPTER 5

Exhibits

Miniature artist Willard Wigan looks through a microscope at one of his own pieces.

78 Mini Marvels

Featured in:
- 2013 book *Download the Weird*
- 2018 anniversary book
  Ripley's Believe It or Not! 100 Years
- Odditoriums around the world

In the late 1800s, the convicted forger A. Schiller was found dead in his cell in New York's infamous Sing Sing prison. The guards found six silver pins and one gold pin on his body. When the precious metal pins were magnified 500 times, all 65 words and 254 letters of the Lord's Prayer were found engraved on the head of each.

The gold pin, with a head 47/1000ths of an inch (1.2 mm) in diameter, is said to be the most perfect example. Schiller had spent 25 years of his life creating the pins, and eventually went blind because of it. Ripley's owns two of the seven Schiller pins; the perfect gold specimen can be found at the St. Augustine, Florida, Odditorium.

Some of the most popular miniature exhibits on display in the Ripley's Odditoriums were created by Willard Wigan from Birmingham, England. These are not just micro-engravings; they are miniscule sculptures that can barely be seen with the naked eye, such as a model of the Statue of Liberty standing inside the eye of a needle.

Some of Wigan's work measures just 0.0002 in (0.005 mm) across, small enough to fit on a grain of sand. In 2011 Ripley's managed to acquire 97 pieces of his work to showcase in their museums, a collection that could probably fit inside a matchbox!

Each artwork can take up to three months to create. Wigan uses custom tools, including shards of diamonds attached to needles, and acupuncture needles. His paintbrushes are eyelashes plucked from his own brows and fine hairs plucked from the back of a housefly.

Wigan's works include a recreation of the great boxing match between Muhammad Ali and Sonny Liston on the head of a pin, a church on a grain of sand, and nine camels inside the eye of a needle. In 2007 Wigan's pinhead-sized replica of the Lloyd's of London building sold for $180,000 and can only be viewed through a microscope.

Wigan goes to great lengths to complete his sculptures. The artist works in a closet just 4 ft (1.2 m) wide to minimize air disturbance, working at night when vibrations

from traffic are at their lowest. He trained himself to improve his powers of concentration, balancing ball bearings on his fingers for hours, and threading hundreds of needles at a time. Now the miniature master can fixate on an artwork for 20 hours straight, working in what he calls a "semi-meditative state."

Wigan holds his breath while he makes alterations, working between heartbeats. Once he held his breath for so long that he passed out. He also once made the mistake of breathing too closely to a work-in-progress, a model of Alice in Wonderland; he inhaled it, and that was that.

Although he must take great care when producing his masterpieces, the finished artworks are surprisingly resilient, and often survive a drop onto the floor. Their small size makes them tough, as the artist explains by comparing them to ants. "If an ant falls off your house roof, it won't die. It's too small."

OUR FATHER WHO ART IN HEAVEN HALLOWED BE THY NAME THY KINGDOM COME THY WILL BE DONE ON EARTH AS IT IS IN HEAVEN GIVE US THIS DAY OUR DAILY BREAD AND FORGIVE US OUR DEBTS AS WE FORGIVE OUR DEBTORS AND LEAD US NOT INTO TEMPTATION BUT DELIVER US FROM EVIL FOR THINE IS THE KINGDOM AND THE POWER AND THE GLORY FOR EVER AMEN

The 47/1000ths-of-an-inch-wide gold pin (1.2-mm) engraved with the Lord's Prayer on display at the St. Augustine, Florida, Odditorium.

79

WE MUST STOP THE KILLING NOW!

Berlin Wall Haul

Featured in:
- 2018 anniversary book *Ripley's Believe It or Not! 100 Years*
- Odditoriums around the world

Ripley's owns 160 ft (48 m) of the Berlin Wall, consisting of 16 graffiti-strewn concrete slabs.

What began as a barbed-wire barricade in 1961 evolved into two parallel 12-ft-high (3.7-m) concrete walls nearly 27 mi (43 km) long with more than 300 guard towers. The zone between the two walls was known as "no man's land" or the "death strip," where guards were able to easily shoot down anyone who dared to cross.

The wall began to come down 28 years later on November 9, 1989, when it was mistakenly announced that East Berliners could cross to the West with zero restrictions, effective immediately. The guards were overwhelmed by the number of people who arrived and began tearing down the wall with pick-axes, sledgehammers, and even their bare hands.

Just three days later, a team from Ripley's went to Germany to see a collection in Hamburg, and later drove to Berlin. Armed with a Swiss army knife, a hammer, and an empty suitcase, they joined a crowd chipping away at the blocks, filling the case with small chunks of concrete. Then they had an idea.

They were able to broker a deal and take much larger sections of the wall, handpicking pieces with striking graffiti art. The 10-ft (3-m) sections were then shipped from Hamburg to America, where they went on display in several Odditoriums.

80

Devil and Damsel

Around 1928, Robert Ripley acquired in Germany a truly remarkable artifact—a double-sided, solid fruitwood statue that depicts the devil on one side and a fair damsel on the other. Incredibly, the statue has been crafted so skillfully that you can never see both figures at the same time.

Featured in:
- Odditoriums around the world
- 2018 book *Odd Is Art*

The life-size statue, standing 5.8 ft (1.8 m) tall, was carved in France in the early 19th century out of a single piece of wood by an unknown sculptor. It depicts two characters from German writer Johann Goethe's 1806 dramatic play *Faust*—the tale of a 16th-century alchemist who, although successful, is dissatisfied with his life and wants more. He decides to sell his soul to the devil in return for a life of pleasure.

In the story, the fair damsel Margaret represents purity and goodness while the Devil, in the shape of Mephistopheles, stands for pure evil. Fittingly, the statue shows the haughty Mephistopheles at the front, dressed in a hooded cloak and wearing a cynical smile, standing back-to-back with the innocent, meek Margaret, who is holding a prayer book. It is traditionally displayed either on a huge turntable or in front of a mirror so that both sides can be viewed.

The legend of Faust was first popularized by English playwright Christopher Marlowe (a contemporary of Shakespeare) with his work *Doctor Faustus*, written sometime between 1589 and 1592. A year after its first performance, Marlowe was murdered. It only became successful after his death, although rumors circulated that during one show, real devils appeared on stage and drove audience members insane.

Goethe's *Faust*, written 200 years later, is considered by many to be the greatest work of German literature and has been translated into numerous languages. The phrases "to sell your soul to the devil" and "to make a pact with the devil" are said to originate from *Faust*.

Robert Ripley and "Cyclops."

Featured in:
- Many cartoons and books over the past century
- Odditoriums around the world

81

Pranks of Nature

ows with six legs, lambs with two faces—these are what Robert Ripley called his "Pranks of Nature," and they are some of the most remarkable exhibits in the Ripley's collection.

Looking like the work of a twisted taxidermist, but 100% natural, the creatures include conjoined piglets, a sheep with two heads, and goats with one eye—a birth defect known as *cyclopia*. Ripley himself joked about owning a one-eyed dog named Cyclops. (In actuality, it was his English sheepdog named Rhumba, whose long hair was cleverly combed to show just one eye.)

An extremely rare two-trunked elephant legally culled in Zimbabwe in 2004.

Lamb with cyclopia.

Eight-legged piglet.

Two-headed boar.

82 Skull Cups

A "Kapala" is a bowl used by Tibetan Buddhists and Indian Hindus in rituals—made from the skulls of Buddhist monks. The skulls are ornately carved or mounted with precious jewels or silver. In religious texts, gods are often portrayed as drinking blood from the ceremonial bowls.

Kapalas are created with skulls salvaged from sacred "sky burial" sites, a Tibetan custom where dead bodies are left out on the hills for the vultures to pick at. Various objects are created from the bones that are left.

There are two types of kapala—those that use the whole skull and those that use only the skull cap or top half of the cranium. They often serve as vessels for holding food or wine, but they are also filled with blood and organs as an offering to the gods, and it's said that some followers also drink blood from the skull cups.

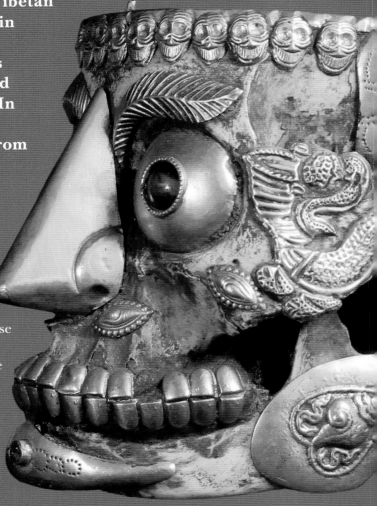

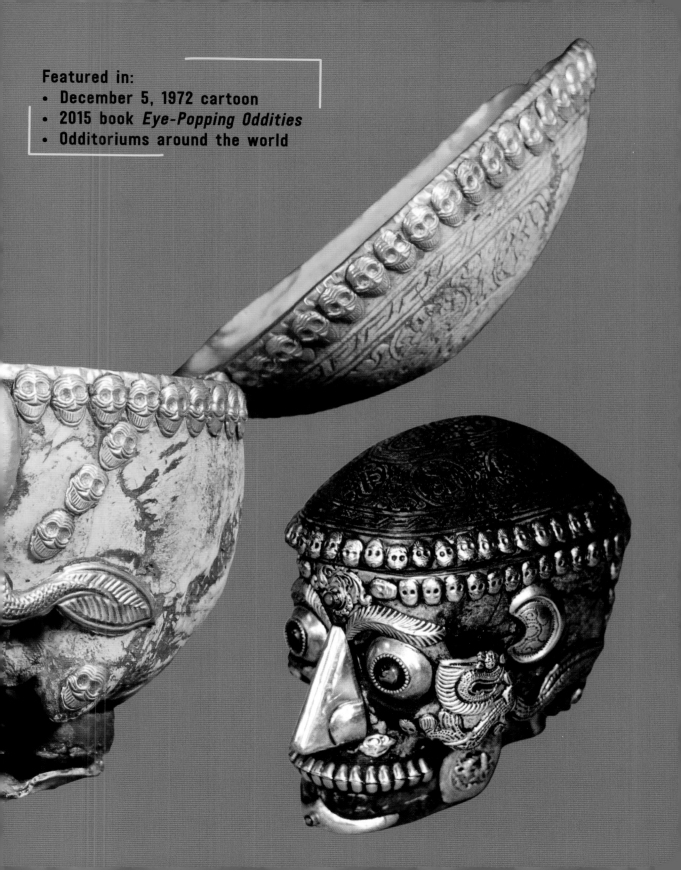

83 Matchstick Man

Patrick Acton of Gladbrook, Iowa, has recreated the Star Wars spaceship Millennium Falcon in matchsticks—more than 900,000 of them! His 15 ft (4.5 m) creation has sound, lighting, and moving parts, and weighs 450 lb (200 kg).

Acton has devoted thousands of hours to his hobby. The career coach spent almost three years building a model of Harry Potter's Hogwarts School, using photographs from the movies as a reference. His detailed replica contains 602,000 matchsticks stuck together with glue. His other matchstick creations include the International Space Station, New York's One World Trade Center, and a moving two-headed dragon.

Acton's largest ever matchstick creation was commissioned by Ripley's in 2015: a winged train built for the New York City Odditorium with more than one million matchsticks and 35 gal (132 l) of wood glue.

Called *Plane Loco*, the train measures more than 20 ft (6 m) long, and 9 ft (3 m) high, and has a wingspan of 13 ft (4 m). It is Acton's own design and took more than 3,000 hours to complete. Guests at Ripley's Times Square Odditorium can play with the train's working headlamp and bell, and use a lever to open the firebox doors.

Millennium Falcon created with 910,000 matchsticks and 26 gal (98 l) of glue!

Two-headed dragon made with more than 273,000 matchsticks! The wings move, the mouths light up, and it even roars!

Featured in:
- October 12, 1992 cartoon
- 2018 book *Odd Is Art*
- Odditoriums around the world

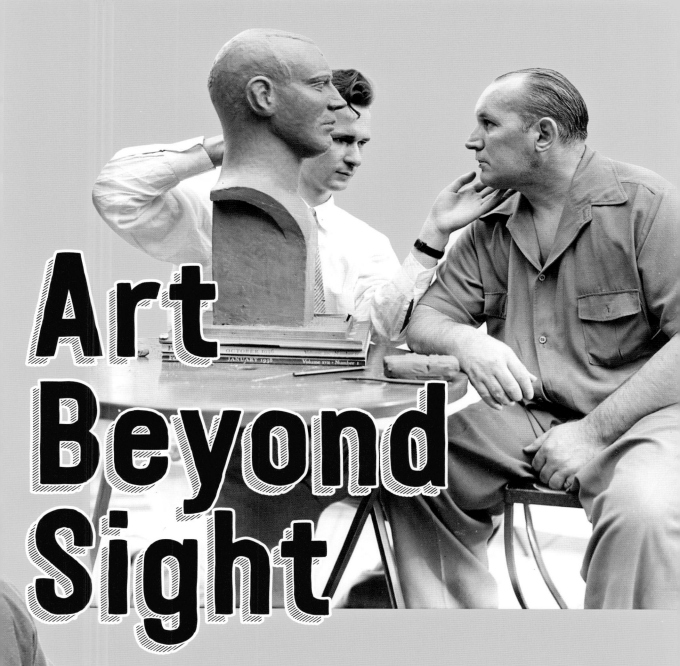

Art Beyond Sight

Mark Shoesmith of New York, seen here with his model, sculpted this bust of Robert Ripley in 1938. Remarkably, Shoesmith was blind and achieved Ripley's likeness purely by touching his face.

Featured in:
- May 25, 1938 cartoon
- 2008 book *Prepare to be Shocked!*
- Odditoriums around the world

Born in Idaho in 1912, Mark Shoesmith was blinded at the age of 12 when the dynamite percussion cap he was playing with exploded in his face. His family enrolled him at a school for the blind in Salem, Oregon, where he tried his hand at sculpting just to find out if he could do it. To his delight, he proved to have a natural talent, and after graduation he did a bust of Lauritz Melchior, a well-known Danish-American tenor at the Metropolitan Opera in New York, as well as the one of Robert Ripley. Unbelievably, Shoesmith had mastered the art of chiseling and whittling compositions out of stone even though he could not actually see what he was doing.

He supplemented his artistic career by teaching at the New York Institute of the Blind before

he and his wife moved to Alamogordo, New Mexico, in 1948. By then his craft had caused so much damage to his hands that he had to give up reading Braille for pleasure.

Another artist who has overcome visual impairment is modern painter Jeff Hanson, of Overland Park, Kansas. Neurofibromatosis and an optic chiasm tumor left him legally blind and he compares his vision to "Swiss cheese." He began his work at the age of 12, when he painted watercolors to pass the time during his chemotherapy sessions. His mother recognized his talent and began using the cards for thank-you notes.

Before long, Jeff was creating large-scale and highly-textured paintings that can be enjoyed by both those with 20/20 vision and people who are completely blind. His inspiring story and impressive pieces garnered the attention of the world, and he sells his paintings for tens of thousands of dollars to buyers like Warren Buffet and Elton John. The profits he generates go to charity; he has currently raised over $3 million and hopes to raise $10 million by the time he turns 30 in 2023!

Featured in:
• **2018 book**
  Odd is Art

Jeff Hanson, the visually impaired artist who created *Road to Odd*.

In 2018, Jeff Hanson created this custom piece just for Ripley's titled *Road to Odd.*

85

Sovereign Slices

Charles, Prince of Wales, married Lady Diana Spencer on July 29, 1981, one of the 20th century's most famous weddings. It's estimated that 750 million people around the world watched the ceremony—more than the last five Super Bowls combined.

Believe it or not, Ripley's has a piece of their wedding cake. A 4-in (10-cm) presentation slice of fruitcake soaked in brandy, the 37-year-old cake is still exquisitely preserved thanks to its high alcohol content.

Already outlasting the royal couple's own marriage by 22 years, this piece of wedding cake has become especially collectible. A similar slice from

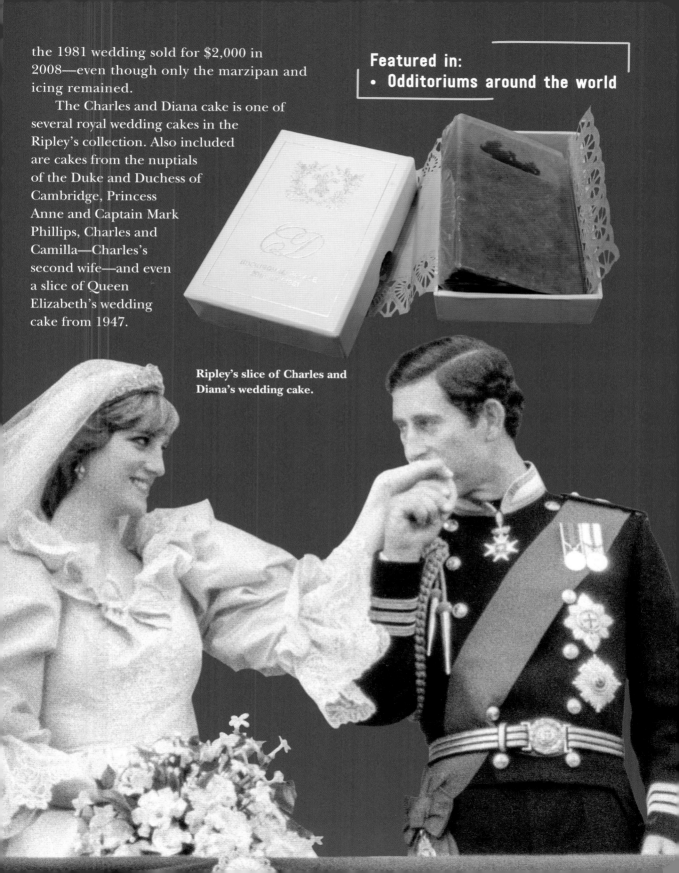

the 1981 wedding sold for $2,000 in 2008—even though only the marzipan and icing remained.

The Charles and Diana cake is one of several royal wedding cakes in the Ripley's collection. Also included are cakes from the nuptials of the Duke and Duchess of Cambridge, Princess Anne and Captain Mark Phillips, Charles and Camilla—Charles's second wife—and even a slice of Queen Elizabeth's wedding cake from 1947.

Ripley's slice of Charles and Diana's wedding cake.

Vampire Killing Kit

This box contains the items considered necessary, for the protection of persons who travel into certain little known countries of Eastern Europe, where the populace are plagued with a particular manifestation of evil known as Vampires. Professor Ernst Blomberg respectfully requests that the purchaser of this kit, carefully studies his book in order, should evil manifestations become apparent, be to that well deal with them efficiently. Professor Blomberg wishes to announce his greatful thanks to that well known gunmaker at Liege, Nicholas Plomdeur whose help in the compiling of the special items, the silver bullets &c., has been most efficient.

The items enclosed are as follows.
(1) An efficient pistol with the usual accoutrements.
(2) Silver bullets.
(3) Crucifix.
(4) Powdered flowers of garlic.
(5) A wooden stake.
(6) Professor Blomberg's new serum.

86

Vampire Killing Kits

There are more than 30 genuine vampire killing kits in the Ripley's archive! In the 19th century, there was a rise in popularity of Eastern European folk stories, particularly the tale of "Vlad the Impaler"—the inspiration for Bram Stoker's 1897 novel *Dracula*. Travelers in that region were sold vampire killing kits containing all that was necessary to vanquish the undead.

A vampire killing kit disguised as a book, containing a pistol, several vials of powders, and a cross.

ne kit in the collection explains its purpose clearly. "This box contains the items considered necessary for the protection of persons who travel into certain little-known countries of Eastern Europe where the populace are plagued with a peculiar manifestation of evil, known as vampires." Many of the kits were said to be made by a Belgian gunmaker called Nicolas Plomdeur, and were sold by Professor Ernst Blomberg (1821–1903) of Lubeck, Germany.

Featured in:
- **2006 book *Expect the Unexpected***
- **Odditoriums around the world**

Vampire killing kits varied in their inventories and value, but there were a few demon-slaying essentials. These included crosses, said to act like kryptonite on vampires; holy bibles; pistols with bullets made of silver; and vials of powder, such as brimstone (sulphur) and potassium nitrate, to be sprinkled around vampire graves to prevent them from rising at night.

Bottles of holy water were popular, and ghoul-repelling garlic in various forms. Some vampire kits contained proprietary serums made from secret ingredients but guaranteed to kill bloodsuckers. And last but not least, almost all kits contained a wooden stake to drive through the beast's heart, preferably made from ash or aspen. For centuries in parts of Europe, bodies were staked through the heart before burial to prevent them from becoming a vampire.

Highlights of the Ripley collection include a vampire killing kit disguised as a book. The fake volume contains a pistol, several vials of powders, and a cross. A particularly gruesome item is a small kit containing a pair of dental pliers with which to remove a vampire's fangs.

Petrified Man

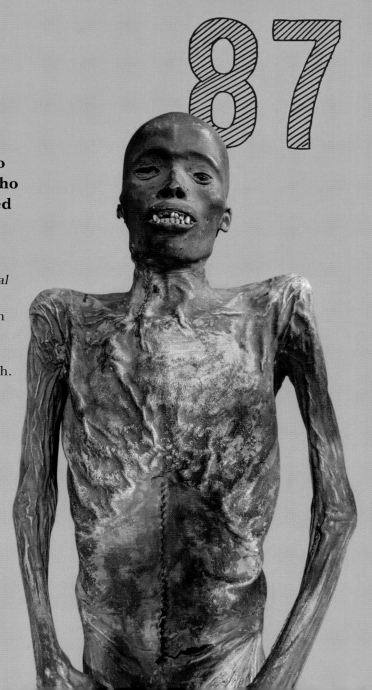

87

"Petrified Man," who lies in the Ripley's collection, is believed to be a Chicago sideshow worker who died in his 30s and was preserved and continued to work for the circus after his death.

The corpse was featured in a *National Geographic* TV show in 2003, and upon inspection he was found to have a nail in his skull, yet he had died from a blow to his chest that punctured his lung and displaced his heart, causing instant death. The scars from his original autopsy, known as "baseball stitching," date this mummy to the 1910s.

Featured in:
- 2003 *National Geographic* TV show *The Mummy Road Show*
- Ripley's exhibit archives

88

President Kennedy's
Birthday Party

MAY 19, 1962
MADISON SQUARE GARDEN

GALA ALL STAR SHOW

END ARENA

SEC.   ROW   SEAT
112

CONTRIBUTION $25. PER PERSON

New York's Birthday Salute To The President, Inc.

SPONSORED BY THE STATE AND NATIONAL DEMOCRATIC
COMMITTEES AND CITIZENS FOR KENNEDY

Dressed To Impress

Ripley's Believe It or Not! has always had a keen eye for the history of pop culture, and on November 17, 2016, it purchased probably the most iconic piece of all—the dress worn by Marilyn Monroe when she sang "Happy Birthday, Mr. President" to John F. Kennedy at New York's Madison Square Garden on May 19, 1962. The dress cost Ripley's more than $5 million, making it the most expensive dress ever bought at auction!

Eager to give the president a 45th birthday to remember—although it was not for another 10 days—Monroe wore the custom-made dress in front of 15,000 guests. Introduced by actor Peter Lawford as the "late Marilyn Monroe" (a dig at her reputation for tardiness), she walked out onto the stage and removed her white ermine fur coat to loud gasps from the audience, because from a distance and under the lights she appeared to be naked.

In fact, she was wearing a skintight, flesh-colored, sheer dress that featured more than 6,000 hand-sewn rhinestones. The dress fabric alone cost a cool $12,000 (equal to more than $95,000 today) and was so tight that it was claimed Monroe had to be sewn into it. She then proceeded to deliver her unforgettably breathy version of the song to serenade the president.

The dress designer was French-born Hollywood costume designer Jean Louis, but the original sketch of the dress was done by none other than a 22-year-old Bob Mackie in his first job out of college. In an interview, he mentioned that he took some inspiration from "dresses where you could see through but not see anything." Bob Mackie went on to dress entertainment icons such as Cher, Bette Midler, Diana Ross, and Judy Garland.

Marilyn was born Norma Jeane Mortenson in Los Angeles in 1926 and married shortly after her 16th birthday. She was working in a California airplane factory in 1944 when photographer David Conover was called in to take propaganda pictures for the war effort and chose young Norma Jeane as a model. Her natural talent prompted Conover to recommend her to a modeling agency.

She straightened her curly brunette hair, dyed it blonde to enhance her appeal, and soon her picture was gracing the covers of a dozen magazines. She earned a movie contract and changed her name to Marilyn Monroe. She would go on to shine in 1950s films such as *Gentlemen Prefer Blondes* and *Some Like It Hot*, but offscreen she led a troubled life.

Less than three months after wowing the world in that dress, Marilyn Monroe was found dead at the age of just 36. Her second husband, baseball star Joe DiMaggio, had half a dozen roses delivered to her grave twice a week for the next 20 years.

Today, everyone still wants a piece of the legend. In addition to the dress, Ripley's owns a lock of her hair, a ring she wore during the filming of *Gentlemen Prefer Blondes*, plus dozens of art pieces featuring her likeness.

89

Mars Rock

On the afternoon of October 3, 1962, a Nigerian farmer was chasing crows from his cornfield near Zagami Rock. Suddenly he heard a loud explosion, the force of which almost knocked him over. Seconds later, an object crashed to the ground amid a cloud of dust about 10 ft (3m) away. Worried that it might be a military shell, the farmer approached cautiously and found a hole about 2 ft (60 cm) deep containing a large black stone. It turned out to be a 40-lb (18-kg) meteorite, and not just any meteorite. This one had just finished a three-million-year journey from Mars.

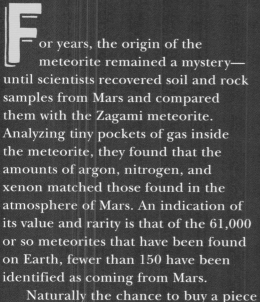

For years, the origin of the meteorite remained a mystery—until scientists recovered soil and rock samples from Mars and compared them with the Zagami meteorite. Analyzing tiny pockets of gas inside the meteorite, they found that the amounts of argon, nitrogen, and xenon matched those found in the atmosphere of Mars. An indication of its value and rarity is that of the 61,000 or so meteorites that have been found on Earth, fewer than 150 have been identified as coming from Mars.

Naturally the chance to buy a piece of Mars was too good for Ripley's to pass up, as Edward Meyer, Ripley's former Vice President of Exhibits and Archives, recalled: "We were at an auction of meteorites in New York City when we were approached by a guy who asked us if we would be interested in a Martian meteorite... We bought the one whole piece for about $50,000. Today it's insured for about $5,000,000."

The Zagami meteorite remains the largest single Mars meteorite ever found. A fragment of it was sent back to Mars on board NASA's Mars Global Surveyor in 1996, making it the first meteorite ever to be returned to space. It is still floating around the red planet on board the now-defunct orbiter, but eventually it will fall onto the surface of Mars to complete its journey home.

Below is the piece of the Zagami meteorite owned by Ripley's, which has since been divided to be shown in multiple Odditoriums around the world.

A Matter of Time

Featured in:
- The San Antonio, Texas, Odditorium
- 2018 book *Odd Is Art*

Paul Baliker of Palm Beach, Florida, specializes in carved sculptures built out of cedar driftwood, finding his medium along the beaches of the Gulf Coast of his home state.

Every year, he creates a piece focusing on the relationship between mankind and nature. *A Matter of Time* is a magnificent carving made entirely from pieces of driftwood found at Florida's Cedar Key. The artwork is 13-ft-tall (4-m) and 13-ft-wide (4-m), featuring 40 animals tangled within the wild mane of mankind. According to Baliker, the piece is a call to action to "take measures right now to quit polluting and destroying natural habitats."

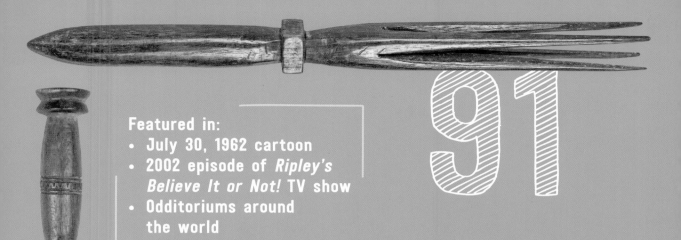

Featured in:
- July 30, 1962 cartoon
- 2002 episode of *Ripley's Believe It or Not!* TV show
- Odditoriums around the world

Cannibal Forks

In 1962, the *Believe It or Not!* cartoon pictured a cannibal fork from Fiji, once known to fearful Western sailors as the "Cannibal Islands." The sharp wooden implement dates from the 18th or 19th century, when cannibalism still played a key part in the warrior culture that had dominated the islands for centuries.

According to gruesome accounts made by Westerners in the 19th century—which may be biased—vanquished enemies would be brought back from the battlefield and ritually eaten as part of a ceremony involving war dances, chanting, and body painting. All of the body was eaten, even the brains.

Cannibal forks were used by tribe members to feed prime cuts of human meat to their chiefs; custom dictated they had to be fed by others during the ritual, and could not be touched. One Fijian chief, Ratu Udre Udre, is thought to have eaten almost 1,000 people, with each one recorded on a stone placed beside his tomb.

Featured in:
- Odditoriums around the world

92 Elephant Armor

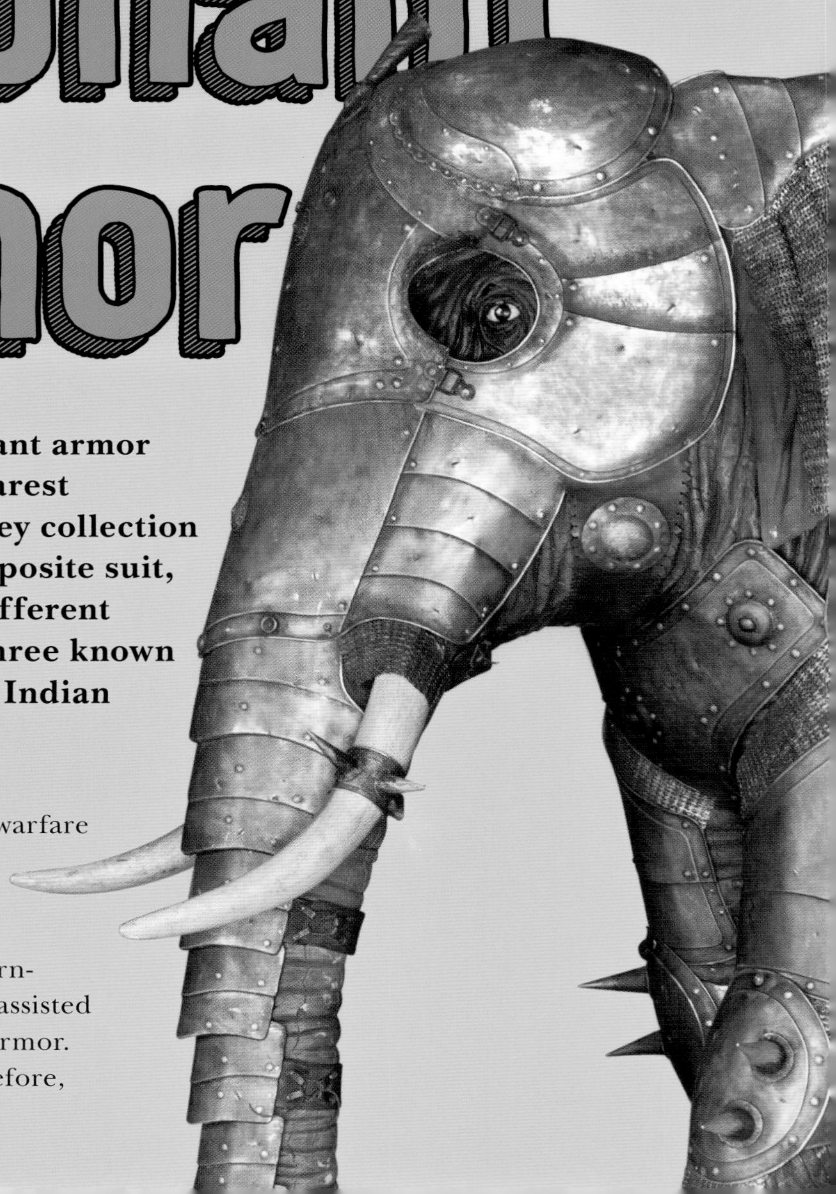

The complete set of elephant armor shown here is one of the rarest artifacts in the entire Ripley collection of oddities. Though a composite suit, made up of pieces from different sources, it is one of only three known complete sets of authentic Indian elephant armor.

Elephants have been used in warfare for more than 2,000 years. In 331 BC, when Alexander the Great fought the Persians at the Battle of Gaugamela in modern-day Iraq, the Persian forces were assisted by 15 elephants wearing suits of armor. Never having seen an elephant before,

Alexander's soldiers were initially terrified of the huge beasts, but still emerged victorious. Five years later, Alexander invaded the Indian territory of Punjab and came up against more than 100 archers and spear throwers riding atop elephants. This time Alexander's troops were not intimidated and were able to capture 80 elephants for use in their own army.

When Hannibal fought the Romans, elephants were again employed to charge the enemy. Elephants' thick skin naturally resisted arrows and spears, so when they wore full armor they were almost invincible, especially when their tusks were fitted with lethal iron spikes. Also, heavy iron balls were often chained to their trunks,

and the animals were trained to swing these around to cause maximum carnage. War elephants would grab soldiers with their trunks, toss them in the air, and then trample them underfoot.

To combat this, the Romans used spiked weapons to injure the elephants' soft foot pads and pots of fire to scare them. This tactic had been practiced during the siege of Megara in 266 BC when the townspeople poured oil on a herd of pigs, set them alight, and drove them toward the enemy's massed war elephants, causing the elephants to flee in terror from the flaming, squealing pigs.

The advent of cannons made elephants less effective in battle, because an animal could easily be felled by a single shot, but in the 17th century the Moghul emperors used war elephants extensively when conquering India. Dressed in full armor, the elephants helped regional rajahs seize even the most fortified towns and villages.

The suit of armor, usually made of steel plates but sometimes padded cloth or leather, covered the elephant's head and back and hung down to the knees. Some were fitted with spiked leg cuffs to help protect the animal's vulnerable legs from ax-wielding warriors. Most suits featured woven face masks that covered the ears and most of the trunk, with holes fashioned for the eyes and tusks. Elephant body armor became a symbol of wealth and power, and was often encrusted with semi-precious stones and jewels and adorned with colorful tassels and golden thread.

An armored elephant made a formidable weapon, and even today strongholds such as Kumbhalgarh Fort in western India still have the spiked gates that were designed to prevent elephants from being used as battering rams.

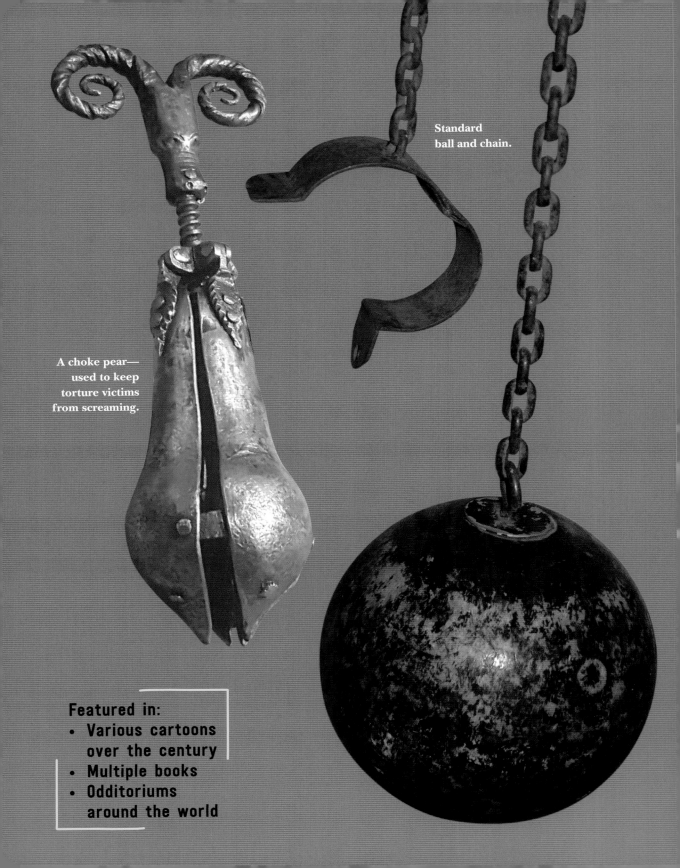

A choke pear—used to keep torture victims from screaming.

Standard ball and chain.

Featured in:
- Various cartoons over the century
- Multiple books
- Odditoriums around the world

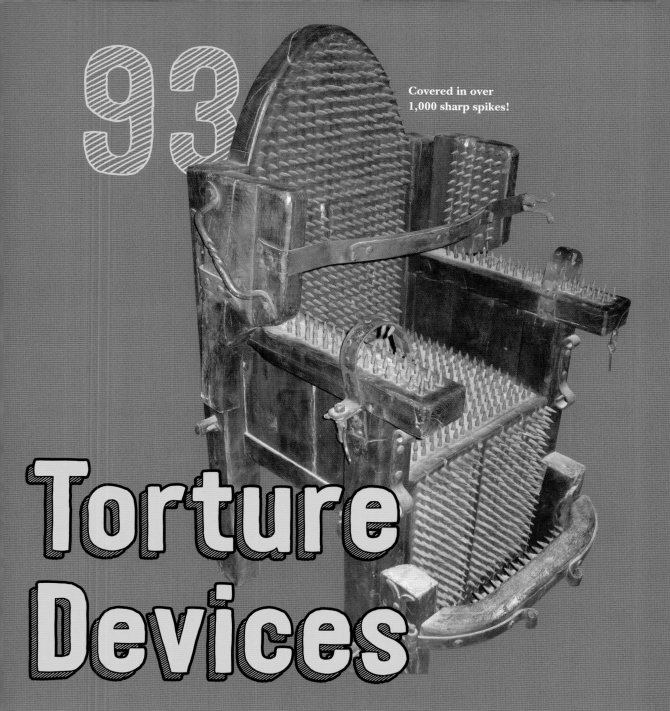

93

Covered in over 1,000 sharp spikes!

Torture Devices

Instruments of torture have been used for centuries to extract confessions from suspects and sinners, and Ripley's has acquired an impressive collection of these devilish devices. Torture was never more widespread than in medieval Europe, where the infamous Spanish Inquisition was established in 1478 to deal with crimes against the all-powerful Catholic Church.

During its three centuries of operation, the Inquisition prosecuted 150,000 people and ordered the execution of 5,000. It employed a range of torture methods, including suspending victims from the ceiling by their wrists, tying heavy metal weights to their ankles, and jerking them violently up and down until their limbs dislocated.

Alternatively, suspects could be beaten mercilessly with a metal flail, which often had a vicious spiked ball attached to the end, or they could be tied to a rack, where their limbs were slowly and painfully pulled apart, or placed in the chair of torture—the Judas Chair. Here, the victim was strapped into a chair that was covered in 1,500 long, sharp metal spikes designed to penetrate the flesh. Death ranged from a few hours to a day or more—unless there was a confession.

Originating in Greece, the torture wheel guaranteed a prolonged and agonizing execution. The victim's limbs were tied to the spokes of a large wooden wheel, which was then slowly revolved. Through the gaps between the spokes, the torturer would lash out with an iron hammer, breaking the victim's bones. It could take three days for him to die of his injuries or dehydration. Sometimes he was strapped to a tall pole so that birds could eat his flesh while he was still barely alive.

Another horrendous device from that period was the choke pear—a pear-shaped metal device that could be inserted into the mouth of a heretic, then screwed open and left there until they suffocated. A 16th-century French robber, Gaucherou de Palioly, is credited with inventing the choke pear to subdue and silence a wealthy Parisian while Palioly and his gang raided his home.

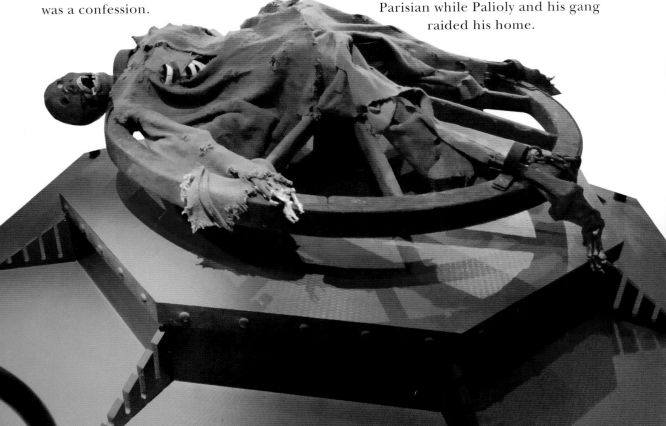

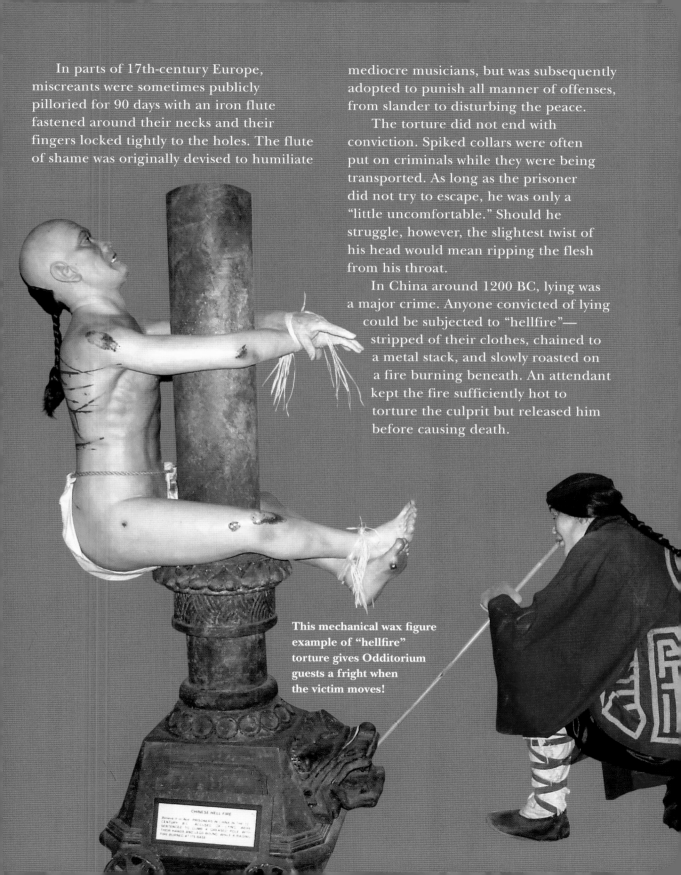

In parts of 17th-century Europe, miscreants were sometimes publicly pilloried for 90 days with an iron flute fastened around their necks and their fingers locked tightly to the holes. The flute of shame was originally devised to humiliate mediocre musicians, but was subsequently adopted to punish all manner of offenses, from slander to disturbing the peace.

The torture did not end with conviction. Spiked collars were often put on criminals while they were being transported. As long as the prisoner did not try to escape, he was only a "little uncomfortable." Should he struggle, however, the slightest twist of his head would mean ripping the flesh from his throat.

In China around 1200 BC, lying was a major crime. Anyone convicted of lying could be subjected to "hellfire"—stripped of their clothes, chained to a metal stack, and slowly roasted on a fire burning beneath. An attendant kept the fire sufficiently hot to torture the culprit but released him before causing death.

This mechanical wax figure example of "hellfire" torture gives Odditorium guests a fright when the victim moves!

CHINESE HELL FIRE

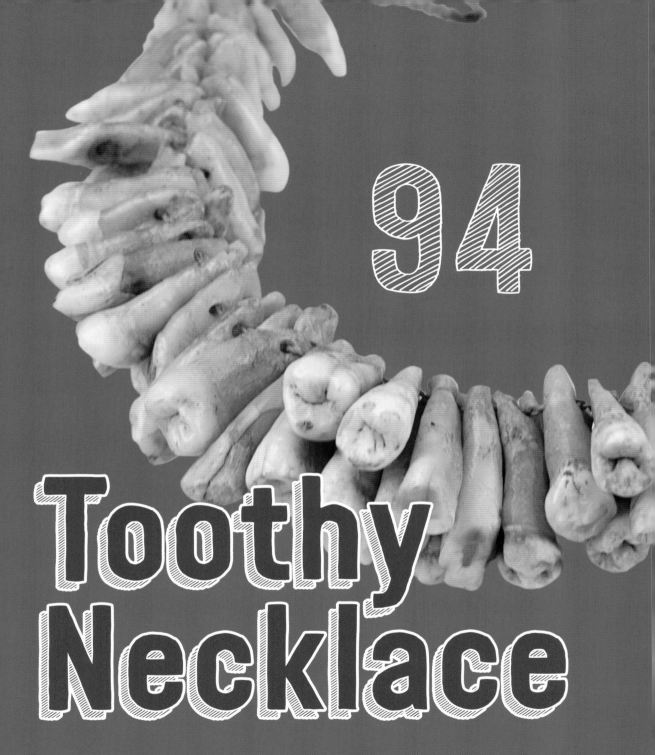

94

Toothy Necklace

When Robert Ripley visited the jungles of New Guinea in 1932, he acquired several cannibal trophies, including a necklace made from 138 human teeth. Since the average human has 32 teeth, the necklace represents at least four eaten people.

murdering someone indiscriminately and taking their head.

To demonstrate their sexual prowess and loyalty to the tribe, Asmat men would butcher a perceived enemy for their kinsmen to eat. After scraping the skin off the head, the baked brains were mixed with sago worms and eaten straight from the halved skulls. The Asmat often used human skulls as pillows for sleeping on at night. They also worshipped the skulls of the deceased. The eyes and the brains were removed and the nasal parts blocked in order to prevent evil spirits from entering or exiting the body, because they believed that once a man is killed and eaten, his powers and skills are transferred to his slayers. These stripped-down skulls were then displayed by the Asmat in a prominent position in their homes. Other body parts, such as the lower jaw, vertebrae, or teeth, were used as trophy jewelry.

The Asmat did not have regular contact with the Western world until the 1970s, and the practice of headhunting is said to have continued into the 1990s until missionaries finally suppressed it. In 1961, Michael Rockefeller, son of future U.S. Vice President Nelson Rockefeller, mysteriously vanished during an expedition into their territory. His body was never found. It is believed he was either killed by crocodiles or slaughtered and eaten by the Asmat.

On arrival in New Guinea, Ripley had been warned not to venture into the jungle because recently a local tribe had invited another tribe to a peace conference, but instead the visitors had slaughtered their hosts—"quartered them and ate their flesh," as Ripley put it. Traditionally the Asmat people of New Guinea were feared headhunters and cannibals. The death of an adult Asmat, even from disease, was believed to be caused by an enemy, and the deceased's relatives sought retribution by

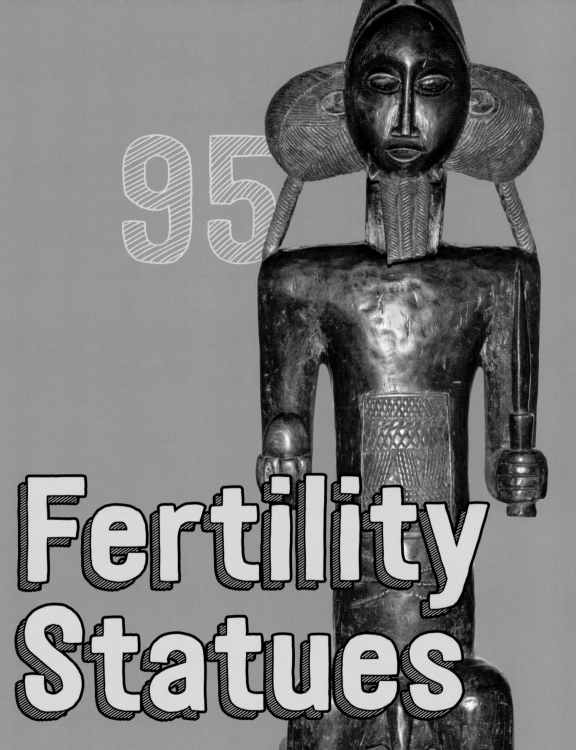

95

Fertility Statues

In 1993 Ripley's acquired two African fertility statues, not realizing they would become one of our most popular exhibits. Thousands of women have testified that after trying to conceive for years, they got pregnant after laying their hands on the legendary statues.

Featured in:
- Odditoriums around the world
- 2004 *Ripley's Believe It or Not!* book
- 2018 book *Odd Is Art*

Believe it or not, when the statues were on display at the Ripley's home office in Orlando, Florida, there were 13 pregnancies in 13 months, mostly among the office staff. News spread quickly and the statues have since toured the world multiple times.

Baulé tribesman of the West African nation of Côte D'Ivoire carved the statues from ebony wood sometime in the 1930s. According to tribal legend, to ensure a couple's fertility, the statues are to be placed on either side of a doorway leading into a bedroom. If a woman or her spouse touches either statue as they enter the room, they will soon get pregnant.

The set includes a male and female, with the woman holding a baby and the man holding a mango and a spear—symbols of fertility. They were hand carved with primitive tools and stand 5 ft (1.5 m) high and weigh more than 70 lb (32 kg) each.

The legend does not specify where one should touch the statues to ensure fertility. For many women, it has not seemed to matter. Thousands of women have testified that after trying to conceive for years, they got pregnant only after laying their hands on the legendary statues. Some have even sent Ripley's photos and scans of their hands so they could touch the statues from a long distance.

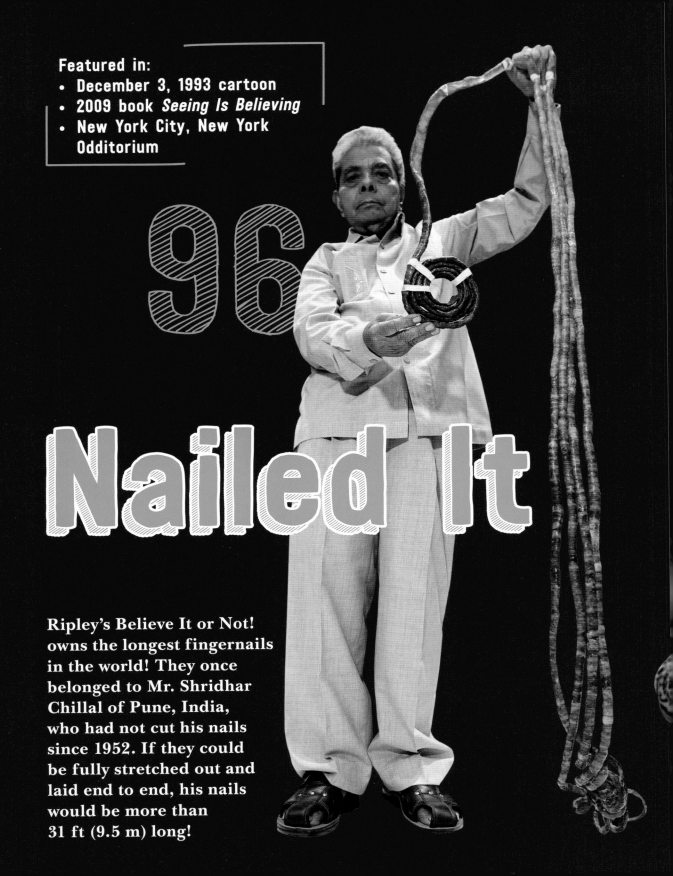

Featured in:
- December 3, 1993 cartoon
- 2009 book *Seeing Is Believing*
- New York City, New York Odditorium

96

Nailed It

Ripley's Believe It or Not! owns the longest fingernails in the world! They once belonged to Mr. Shridhar Chillal of Pune, India, who had not cut his nails since 1952. If they could be fully stretched out and laid end to end, his nails would be more than 31 ft (9.5 m) long!

Mr. Chillal decided to grow his nails when he was scolded by his school teacher as a result of accidentally breaking the teacher's long nail. The teacher said that Chillal would never understand the importance of what he had done because Chillal had never committed to anything. "I took it as a challenge," said Chillal, and there was no looking back.

Mr. Chillal's unusual choice didn't stop him from leading a normal and happy life. He married, has two children, three grandchildren, and enjoyed a successful career as a government press photographer. However, as he aged, his long nails made it more and more challenging to maintain an ordinary lifestyle. He found it difficult to sleep, and even a gust of wind was cause for alarm. He only grew the nails on his left hand; his right hand's nails are trimmed. Due to years of growing his nails and the weight of the nails, his hand is permanently handicapped—he cannot open his hand from a closed position or flex his fingers. At the age of 82, he decided to finally shorten the nails on his left hand.

In 2018, Ripley's flew Mr. Chillal from India to the United States to cut his nails and forever memorialize them in Ripley's Believe It or Not! Times Square Odditorium. Believe it or not, a rotary tool was needed to cut through the nails!

Chillal was not alone in his endeavor. Previously featured in the 2014 book *Ripley's Believe It or Not! Reality Shock!* was Ayanna Williams of Houston, Texas. The most recent measurement of her nails in 2017 put them at a combined length of 18 ft 11 in (5.8 m). She devotes several hours a day tending to her nails, which are capped—painted on the top and around the edges—to help prevent breakage. Ayanna has no intention of cutting them, saying "I love them. They are 50% of who I am. To cut them would be like losing a limb."

Featured in:
- **2014 book**
  Reality Shock!

97 Pop Culture Collection

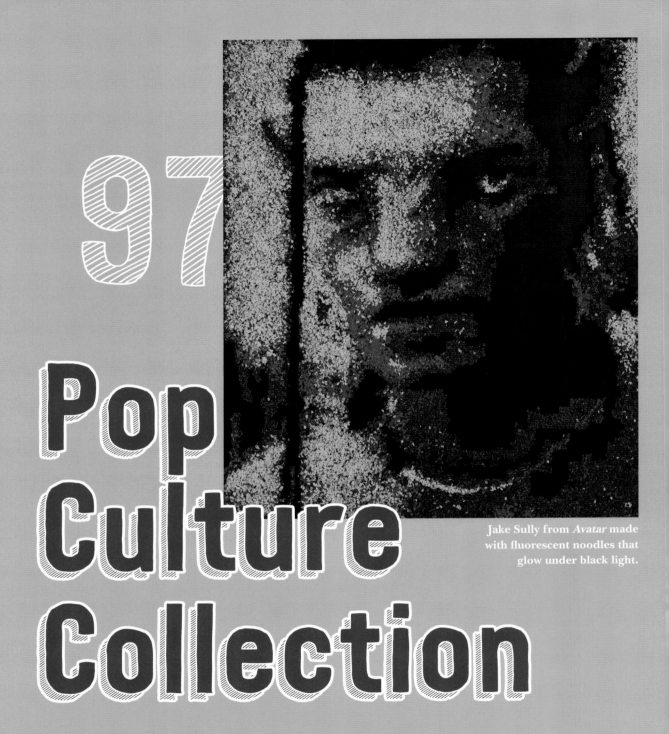

Jake Sully from *Avatar* made with fluorescent noodles that glow under black light.

There are more than 30,000 objects in the Ripley's Believe It or Not! archives, ranging from taxidermied pranks of nature to medieval torture devices, but also included are pieces of pop culture history, giving guests an intimate look at the props used to make their favorite movies, music videos, TV series, and more.

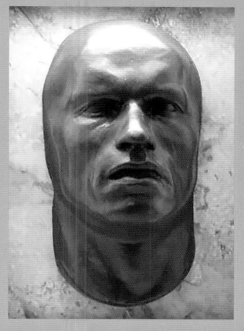

A mold of Arnold Schwarzenegger's face, also known as a "life mask."

A scene from *Alice in Wonderland* created with the text of the first four chapters of the book. Artist Rick Almanson is left-handed and had to write upside-down to avoid smudging the letters.

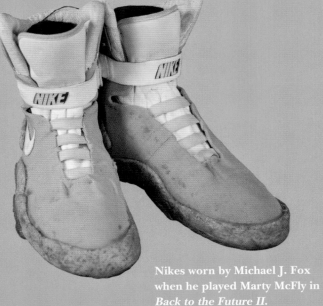

tems from worldwide phenomena like Star Wars, *Ben-Hur*, *Indiana Jones*, *Chitty Chitty Bang Bang*, *Jaws*, *King Kong*, and others have found their way into Odditoriums around the world. Pop culture pieces like the ones shown here give fans a relatable touchstone among the rest of the unbelievable exhibits.

In addition to props, there are autographs, personal items, wax figures, life masks, and also thousands of art pieces paying tribute to famous people and media, usually created with unlikely materials. Believe it or not, we even own a pair of Madonna's underwear!

Nikes worn by Michael J. Fox when he played Marty McFly in *Back to the Future II*.

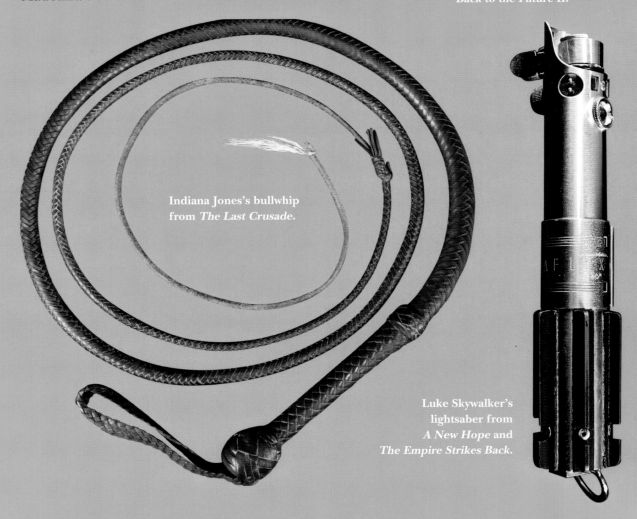

Indiana Jones's bullwhip from *The Last Crusade*.

Luke Skywalker's lightsaber from *A New Hope* and *The Empire Strikes Back*.

Larger than life bust of Janis Joplin by Ivan Lovatt made entirely out of galvanized chicken wire.

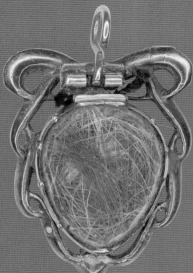

A brooch with both George and Martha Washington's hair

A snippet of Napoléon Bonaparte's hair. While never a U.S. president, he was president of the Italian Republic from 1802 to 1805.

98
Presidential Hair

Long before autographs and selfies, the custom in the 19th century was to collect locks of hair from famous dead people. Robert Ripley continued the trend, acquiring a framed sample of U.S. President Andrew Jackson's hair among others, and hair auctions are still popular today, with a lock of Abraham Lincoln's hair, taken on his deathbed, valued at more than $500,000.

Lincoln's is arguably the most poignant of the Ripley's Believe It or Not! presidential hair exhibits. When Lincoln was shot on the evening of April 14, 1865, at Ford's Theatre in Washington, D.C., the dying president was taken across the street to the bedroom of a small boarding house, which, ironically, had been visited a few months before by his assassin, John Wilkes Booth.

Three surgeons attended, including Dr. Charles Sabin Taft, who was in the audience at the theatre and had rushed to the stricken president's box. Taft trimmed Lincoln's hair in an attempt to remove the bullet, but it quickly became apparent that there was no hope of saving him.

That fateful lock of hair has since been sub-divided many times, and Ripley's owns a strand, displayed with a small fragment of the United States flag that hung from the funeral train carrying Lincoln's body from Washington back to Springfield, Illinois, for burial.

Other strands of Lincoln's hair, clipped by Dr. Taft during the autopsy, were used to form expertly crafted images of the president's log cabin birthplace for display in a Victorian locket and brooch—one of the earliest examples of hair art.

Ripley's collection also includes a lock of First Lady Mary Lincoln's hair, a letter and lock of hair from George Washington, plus strands from the heads of John F. Kennedy and Ronald Reagan. JFK's hair was sold to Ripley's by his personal barber, Harry Gelbart, and believe it or not, strands of Kennedy's hair are rarer than George Washington's.

Ripley's hair collection doesn't stop at presidents, however. Inside the archives is a tuft of hair from the King of Rock and Roll himself— Elvis Presley.

A locket featuring President Abraham Lincoln's hair shaped into a log cabin.

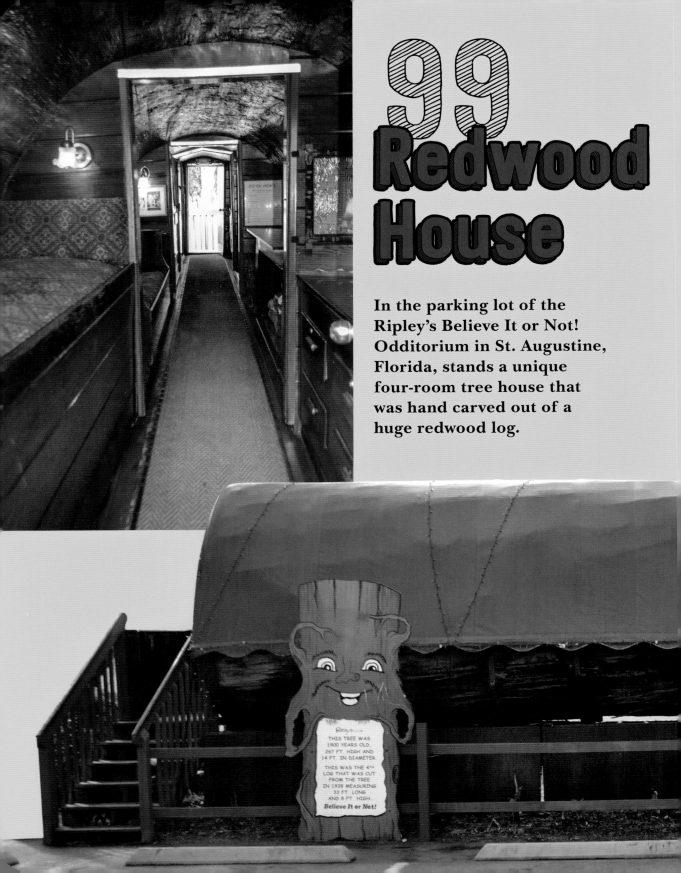

99 Redwood House

In the parking lot of the Ripley's Believe It or Not! Odditorium in St. Augustine, Florida, stands a unique four-room tree house that was hand carved out of a huge redwood log.

THIS TREE WAS 1900 YEARS OLD. 267 FT. HIGH AND 14 FT. IN DIAMETER.

THIS WAS THE 4TH LOG THAT WAS CUT FROM THE TREE IN 1938 MEASURING 33 FT. LONG AND 8 FT. HIGH.

Believe It or Not!

Len Moore, of Eureka, California, first had the idea for creating a house from a hollowed-out tree when he took shelter in a fallen, burned-out redwood during a storm and realized that there was enough room to live there. Starting in 1938, he built his dream home from a section of a 267-ft-tall (81-m), 14-ft-diameter (4.3-m) coastal redwood tree that was about 1,900 years old.

The log he used was the fourth cut from the tree and measured 33 ft (10 m) long and 8 ft (2.4 m) high, giving him plenty of headroom. It contains more than 11,000 board-feet of lumber, enough to build a five-bedroom house.

It took Moore four months to chisel out the interior of the log and over a year to build. He lived in the house for eight years, and it later became home to several owners before being acquired for the first permanent Ripley's Believe It or Not!

Odditorium, which had opened in St. Augustine in 1950, a year after Robert Ripley's death. Ripley's collection is housed in the former Castle Warden hotel, where Ripley himself had been a guest on several occasions.

Built in 1887, the building is rumored to be haunted by the ghosts of Ruth Hopkins Pickering and Betty Neville Richeson, who died in a fire at Castle Warden in 1944. According to local legend, they were actually murdered first and their bodies burned to conceal the crime. Since then, a number of Ripley's employees say they have seen or heard the ghosts of the two women, a story recounted in the Ripley's Ghost Train Adventure, which shows the ghosts peering eerily out of the windows of their rooms.

Featured in:
- **St. Augustine, Florida, Odditorium**

Featured in:
- April 15, 2008 cartoon
- Odditoriums around the world
- 2006 book *Expect the Unexpected*
- 2018 book *Odd Is Art*

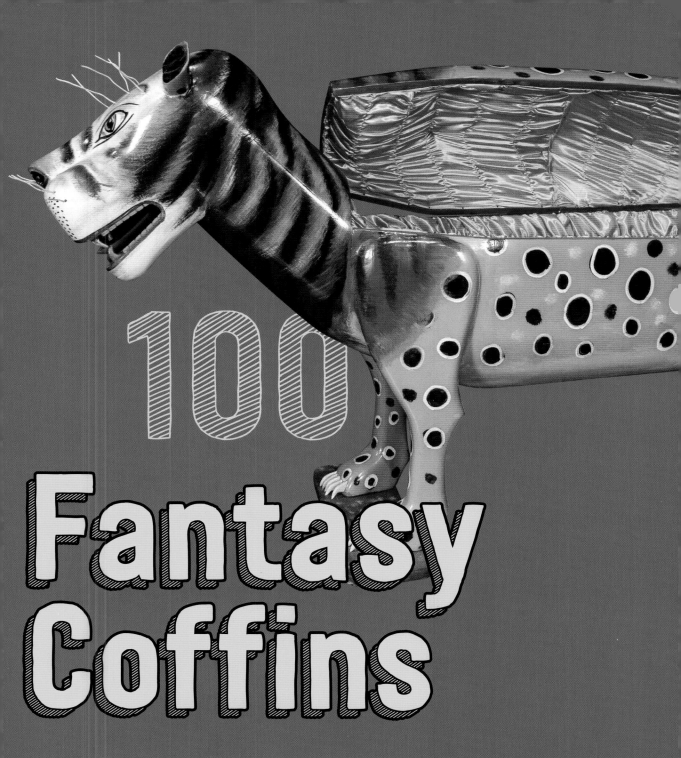

100
Fantasy Coffins

Instead of being buried in plain wooden coffins, people who die in the African country of Ghana are often laid to rest in ornate, hand-made caskets that come in the shape of anything, including a Coca-Cola bottle, a lobster, a pineapple, a shoe, or an elephant.

Each fantasy coffin is custom-made to reflect an element of the deceased—such as their occupation, personality, or standing in the community. A cab driver might be buried in a car-shaped coffin, a farmer could be placed inside a rooster, and a priest or a member of royalty would warrant a coffin in the design of a sword or a throne. The head of the family or a tribal chief is often buried in a lion-shaped casket.

The tradition for designer coffins began in Accra in the 1950s with master craftsmen such as Ataa Oko and Seth Kane Kwei, and has been widely adopted by the Ga people of southern Ghana, who believe that their loved ones continue into another world when they die. They also believe that ancestors are all-powerful and are able to influence those who are still alive on Earth. Families go to great lengths to ensure that a dead person will look favorably upon them as quickly as possible, and the best way to do that is to give the deceased an extravagant funeral procession lasting for up to three days and nights.

Consequently, they will often spend $600 on a special coffin, which, for some, is equal to a year's salary. The coffins are produced to order, using only the simplest tools, without the aid of any electrical appliances. Each one can take up to six weeks to make.

Today one of Ghana's leading coffin artists is Paa Joe, who began his apprenticeship in the workshop of Kane Kwei. Some of his coffins are shipped abroad as works of art. In 2014, one of Joe's coffins in the shape of a Porsche sold at auction in London for $9,200. Ripley's has bought a number of his creations—including caskets in the shape of a cobra, a leopard, and a butterfly—for exhibition around the world.

One of his craziest orders was for a Chevrolet Stingray convertible coffin with room for two people. Two of his coffins were reportedly bought by former U.S. President Jimmy Carter.

"GO" IN STYLE!

MANY CRAFTSMEN IN GHANA, WEST AFRICA CREATE COFFINS IN THE SHAPE OF FOODS, ANIMALS, VEHICLES AND OTHER OBJECTS THAT SYMBOLIZE THEIR CUSTOMER'S LIFESTYLE!

Acknowledgments

Cover and chapter openers Jes2ufoto/Alamy Stock Photo 1.4 (br) Kevin Winter/Getty Images 3.1 Bettmann via Getty Images 3.2 Eddie Jackson/NY Daily News Archive via Getty Images 3.3 (l) Bettmann via Getty Images 7.2 The History Collection/Alamy Stock Photo 9.3 Bettmann via Getty Images 12.1 © Hulton-Deutsch Collection/CORBIS/Corbis via Getty Images 13.1-2 © Roger Ressmeyer/CORBIS/VCG via Getty Images 15.4 Ira Berger/Alamy Stock Photo 19.2 (tr) © Hulton-Deutsch Collection/CORBIS/Corbis via Getty Images 20.1-2 © Everett Historical/Shutterstock.com 23.2 (bl) Bob Landry/The LIFE Picture Collection/Getty Images; (tr) AP Photo/David Zalubowski 28.1 Geoff Robinson Photography/REX/Shutterstock 28.2 (b) Geoffrey Robinson/REX/Shutterstock 30.1 Bettmann via Getty Images 30.2 Tom Watson/NY Daily News via Getty Images 30.3 Bettmann via Getty Images 31.1 AP Photo 33.1 Courtesy of Sony Pictures Television. All rights reserved. 34.1 ART Collection/Alamy Stock Photo 35.1 James Devaney/WireImage via Getty Images 36.2 (bl) ullstein bild/ullstein bild via Getty Images 38.3 (t) AP Photo/Cyrena Chang; (b) AP Photo/Mike Albans 41.1 Cover Asia Press/ Faisal Magray 43.1 William England/Getty Images 43.2 Hulton Archive/Getty Images 45.1-4 GEORGE VLOSICH/CATERS NEWS 48.1 Photo by Rafaela Ferraz (rafaelaferraz.com) 48.2 (tr) ullstein bild/ullstein bild via Getty Images 49.1 Image via Sideshow World 49.2 Public Domain {{PD-US}} http://www.angelfire.com/art/rapunzellonghair/rapunzellonghairarchive/portrait4.htm 51.1 Anglia Press Agency Ltd./REX/Shutterstock 51.3 Bettmann via Getty Images 52.2 Richard Ellis/Alamy Stock Photo 53.1 Stephen Hopkins/Rex Features 58.1 PC - Jeff Erickson 59.2 Chronicle/Alamy Stock Photo 60.1 Michael Goldman/The LIFE Images Collection/Getty Images 61.1 Gary Miller/Getty Images 62.2 Travel Pictures/Alamy Stock Photo 64.3 (tl) Parramatta Veterinary Hospital/Caters News; (br) Animal Referral Hospital Sydney/Caters News 65.1 MARK RALSTON/AFP/Getty Images 66.1-2 Caters News 67.1-2 Images courtesy of Boaz Rottem 68.2 Images & Stories/Alamy Stock Photo 72.1 studioEAST/Getty Images 72.2 (t) LUDOVIC MARIN/AFP/Getty Images 74.1 Chester Voyage/Alamy Stock Photo 75.1-2 Phillip Bond/Alamy Stock Photo 75.3-4 Bettmann via Getty Images 76.1 ABIR ROY BARMAN/Alamy Stock Photo 76.2 Kaveh Kazemi/Getty Images 79.2 Peter Timm\ullstein bild via Getty Images 84.3 Jeffrey Owen Hanson www.JeffHansonArt.com 85.1 David Levenson/Getty Images 85.2 (b) Alisdair MacDonald/Daily Mirror/Mirrorpix/Getty Images 88.4 Bettmann via Getty Images 89.1 Public Domain {{PD-US}} NASA 89.2 (t) Public Domain {{PD-US}} NASA/JPL/USGS 90.1 Paul A. Baliker

Key: t = top, b = bottom, c = center, l = left, r = right, dp = double page, bkg = background. Numbers refer to the story and on which page of that story an image appears.

All other photos are from the Ripley's Believe It or Not! archives.

Stop by our website daily for new stories, photos, contests, and more!
www.ripleys.com

 /RipleysBelieveItOrNot @Ripleys

 youtube.com/Ripleys @RipleysBelieveItorNot

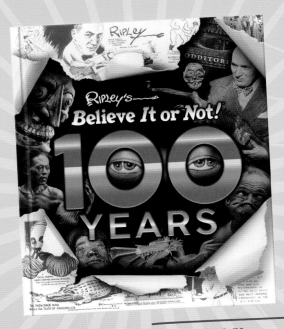

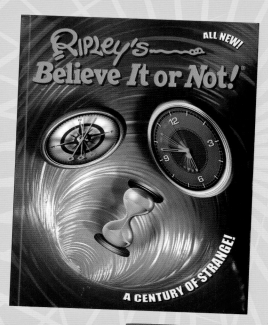

Ripley's Believe It or Not! 100 Years
Go beyond the BION in this book celebrating the history of Ripley's with never-before-seen archival photos, behind the scenes anecdotes, and stunning bonus features, such as removable replicas and gatefolds.

A Century of Strange!
Over 1,200 new and unbelievable stories! See lava that glows blue at night, marvel at the balancing skills of a bicycle ballerina, and try not to cringe at the sight of a face-hugging bug! All this and more inside *A Century of Strange!*

Time Warp
Get ready to have your mind blown by this incredible collection of events, inventions, and people that you won't believe existed at the same time in history!

Ripley's Believe It or Not! Graphic Novel
See amazing Ripley stories in a brand-new way in this 96-page anthology, written and illustrated by a mix of comic book legends and rising stars.